Christian Denominations

Christian Denominations

By

Rev. Vigilius H. Krull,
C.PP.S., LL.B.

Fourteenth Edition

M. A. Donohue & Co.

Chicago, Illinois

IMPRIMI POTEST.

    IG. A. WAGNER, C.PP.S.

NIHIL OBSTAT.

    AUGUSTINUS SEIFERT, C.PP.S.

IMPRIMATUR.

    ✠ HERMAN JOSEPHUS,
        Episcopus Wayne Castrensis
        Wayne Castris, die 22 Julii 1911

    ✠ JOSEPHUS SCHREMBS,
        Episcopus Clevelandensis
        Cleveland, Ohio, March 19, 1925

    ✠ CAROLUS ALTER,
        Episcopus Toletanus
        Toledo, Ohio, Oct. 22, 1935.

COPYRIGHT, 1936

REV. V. H. KRULL, C.PP.S.

MANUFACTURED IN THE UNITED STATES OF AMERICA

Introduction

IN offering this book to the public, I purpose to furnish my readers with a brief, but reliable exposition of the history and teachings of the different Christian denominations found in this country; the names of the various founders together with a short sketch of their work and views; the time of the origin and the main teachings and practices of the many Christian denominations. The extensive extracts from the works of the Fathers and other ecclesiastical writers of the early Church will undoubtedly be of interest to the earnest Christian.

With the help of God's grace and the aid of Holy Scripture and sound reason, turning the flash-light of true history upon every organization mentioned in this book, we can easily detect and distinguish the true Church, which Jesus Christ, the Son of God, founded, from any and every purely human institution. "Seek and you shall find."

If this book brings my readers nearer to Jesus, "who loved us, and washed us from our sins in His blood," I consider my work amply repaid.

THE AUTHOR.

Foreword to the Fourteenth Edition
"Christian Denominations"

→»«←

IN the fourteenth edition the membership of the various denominations has been revised in accord with the most recent statistics available. A few eliminations, corrections and changes were made.

Paragraphs on "Sound Reasoning Leads to God" and "Jesus, the Son of God" have been embodied.

In other words, "Christian Denominations" not only gives the history and the teachings of the various denominations and their number of adherents but it also contains some natural proofs for the existence of God and biblical proofs for the divinity of Jesus Christ, the Founder of Christianity. Now the book is up-to-date.

Previous to the fourteenth edition, thirty-five thousand copies of "Christian Denominations" have been scattered over the world. May this edition help to bring the hearts and minds of my readers nearer to Jesus, who redeemed us by His Precious Blood.

Jan. 12, 1936.   THE AUTHOR.

Table of Contents

	PAGE
Introduction	v
Foreword to the Fourteenth Edition	vii
Statistics on Religion	1
Sound Reasoning Leads to God	4
Jesus the Son of God	17
The Catholic Church	25
Chronological List of Roman Pontiffs	63
The Seven Sacraments	68
The Holy Sacrifice of the Mass	88
The Blessed Virgin Mary	95
Synopsis of Catholic Doctrines	103
Greek Orthodox Church	112
Lutheran Church	115
Anglican or Episcopal Church	136
Presbyterian Church	142
Congregational Church	149
Anabaptists	154
The Mennonite Church	159
The Baptist Church	162
Moravians or Bohemian Brethren	176
Friends or Quakers	179
The Methodist Church	182
United Brethren in Christ	188
Adventists	193

Contents — concluded

	PAGE
Christian Catholic Church of Zion-Dowieites	196
Salvation Army	206
Mormons or Latter Day Saints	209
Universalists	216
Unitarians	219
Church of the New Jerusalem	222
Church of Christ, Scientist	228
Concluding Remarks	233
Index Alphabetically Arranged	237

Statistics on Religion in the World Today

UPON the command of His Holiness Pope Pius XI a CATHOLIC WORLD ATLAS was prepared and published in the year 1929. This was done by F. C. Streit for the Society for the Propagation of the Faith. This book contains a geographical and statistical description with maps of the Holy Roman Catholic Church. The exact number of Catholics in the various parts of the world are given.

We summarize the number of Catholics
in United States, Mexico, Canada,
Central and South America........199,096,603
All Europe 208,991,598
All Asia 16,535,812
All Africa 5,329,455
Australia and Islands...........1,584,541

Total number of Catholics........431,428,009

There is no doubt in my mind that the above figures are correct.

For the statistics of the rest of religious denominations the sources of information are not so exact and reliable.

In the first group of the religious membership of

the world I mention Jews and Christians. They are believers in the one true God. There is but one God. We Christians profess upon the authority of the Son of God that in the one true God there are three Divine Persons, namely, the Father, the Son and the Holy Ghost. We find that the Father, the Son and the Holy Ghost have the same divine nature. This doctrine is called the Blessed Trinity: three divine and distinct Persons in the one and the same God.

Those who believe in the one true God and His Ten Commandments are:

Jews	16,000,000
Catholics	431,428,009
Greek Orthodox	127,000,000
Protestants	171,000,000
Total	745,428,009

Other religions in the world are:

Mohammedans	219,000,000
Buddhists	135,000,000
Hindus	210,000,000
Confucianists	301,000,000
Shintoists	21,000,000
Animists	136,000,000
Total	1,022,000,000

The above total are neither Jews nor Christians. The total number of believers in
God are 1,767,428,009

Statistics on Religion in the World Today

The number of people in the world according to the *Catholic World Atlas* of 1929 is 1,940,744,350
Deduct the number of believers 1,767,428,009

from the total number of people in the world and we find, if figures are correct, that there are 173,316,341

unbelievers or people without religion in the world today.

It is high time that Jews and Christians unite in an effort to enlighten those who are without any belief and knowledge of God. Profess your belief in God publicly. It is the knowledge and the practice of truth that dispels error and deplorable ignorance. We believe in God; we hope in God, and we love God. These facts we must not hide from our fellowmen. The Ten Commandments of God are and must be the norm of our human acts.

N.B. Instead of accounting for the existence of the world by acknowledging the omnipotence of God, the Creator of heaven and earth, many people assume that the world came into existence by mere chance and fictitious evolution.

Sound Reasoning Leads to God

➤➤➤ ⋘⋘⋘

THERE are quite a number of persons in this country who do not practice any religion. They are not members of any church. They imagine that religion is based upon sentimentality.

Many of these persons would practice religion if they could find any reason for doing so. They do not know that there are sound basic proofs for the existence of God, for the divinity of Christ, and for the mission of the true Church. Perhaps you come in contact with some of these unbelievers. You may help them by acquainting them with the proofs contained in this booklet. Sound reasoning leads to God. The examples adduced in the argumentation on the existence of God are suggestive of similar examples. The reader should use similar arguments and follow this same method of reasoning. We use the example of a watch to prove that there is a watchmaker. We may also use the example of a shoe to prove that there is a shoemaker, or the example of a wagon to prove that there is a wagon maker. All of this may be used as a means to realize the fact that every effect has a cause. When we behold a thing we know that that thing was caused by something or somebody. When we see a thing in motion we know that somebody or something started the thing to move. The whole universe is in motion. Who started it to move? The Prime-mover is God.

Who is God and Where is He?

1. *Cause and Effect*

THAT watch was made. You know that it did not come together by itself. Perhaps you have never met the man who made it. Nevertheless you know that some one made the watch, and that it would be foolish to say: "I don't believe that anyone made my watch, because I did not see it." How do you know then that there is a watchmaker and has been one, though you never saw him? You know it by the watch which was made. By the thing made we prove that there must be a maker. In other words, by the effect we argue the cause.

Look about in nature. No matter whither we look, we see how one thing is caused by another. The change of weather, the recurrence of the seasons, the sprouting of the flower, the birth among animals, the numerical growth of mankind; all of these are effects produced by their respective causes. There is a cause for everything. Now, all these things, as we observe, have a beginning and come to an end. We are all finite beings. There was a time when neither you nor I existed. None of us existed a hundred years ago. There was a time when our parents did not as yet exist, neither their parents, nor any of their ancestors. Thus going back from parent to parent, we come to a period when no human being existed. The first man had no parents.

How did he come into existence? He could not make himself, because he did not exist. No human being existed; therefore, some one else was the cause of his coming into existence. The First Cause of man's existence we call God. God created man.

The First Cause of all created things we call God. Trace the pedigree of an animal to the utmost. Finally, we behold the first. That first animal evidently was not born. How did it come into existence?

Take the trees. Some of them developed from the planted seed. That seed came from another tree; that tree from another seed, and so on and on until we come to the first tree. It could not come by itself. Who caused that tree to be? That First Cause we call God.

God is the First Cause of all created beings; God is our Creator. He gave us existence and caused all things by which we are kept alive. God is He who gave us being and life and keeps us in existence, keeps us alive. He is the author of our being and of all the good in existence.

From the existence of finite beings, going back to the start, we come to the knowledge of an infinite self-existent Being, the creator of all; we come to the knowledge of God. Moreover we come to the knowledge that He who brought beings into existence must be omnipotent, all-powerful; and that He must exist independent of creation, an all-sufficient, intelligent, eternal, perfect Being. Reason tells us before the world was made, or anything was in it, God existed. Therefore He does not depend upon the things which He created.

Sound Reasoning Leads to God

2. Motion and Moving Power

An automobile speeds along the road, or a majestic passenger train runs at a tremendous rate. You see it and admire the speed. You know for certain that neither the train nor the auto started by itself. You know that someone set it into motion. Motion presupposes a mover, no matter who or what that may be. By itself nothing can move which belongs to inanimate nature. Motion is the effect of a moving cause. All the world is in motion; and all that is in it moves along with it through space immeasurable. The stir of a soft evening breeze as well as the howling hurricane indicates motion. The light of the sun, which we see every day, is another proof of great motion. Light travels at the tremendous speed of 186,000 miles a second. The clouds in the sky, the stars in the firmament are moving along continually. Even the tiny blade of grass by its slow growth is in motion. Growth, be it ever so slow, is in motion. From the remotest heavenly planets to the most humble creature on earth, motion is everywhere. We behold the earth vibrating and pulsating from end to end, from day to day, from year to year, incessantly in motion. If we reflect for a moment, we understand plainly that there must be one, who caused the first motion; and this Primemover we call God. One thing moves another; but the first thing could not move unless it was put into motion. The motion in the world argues a Primemover, proclaims the existence and action of God, in whom "we live and move and are." Acts 17:28.

3. Necessity and Contingency

The answer to the question, who is God? may be this: God is the necessary Being. That sounds rather philosophical. It means the same as saying: God must exist and does exist; the universe may exist and does exist. Real truth always excludes error. In this, mathematical and metaphysical truth are alike. Nevertheless, there is a vast difference between our perception of truth. We know that some statements are so evidently true that they cannot be otherwise; two times two must be four. That is a necessary fact. We cannot even think it to be otherwise.

Now I give you another fact. Here is the statement: Chicago is built near Lake Michigan. This is a fact, but we can easily see that Chicago might have been built somewhere else. That the world exists is a contingent fact. Anything in the world occupies space for a while. There is a tree in the field. That is a contingent fact only, for we see instantly that it might be otherwise. Thus it is with every part of the universe; and what is true of its constituent parts is true of the whole universe. The existence of the world is a contingent fact. A contingent fact always presupposes a cause, which determined it so. The world exists, but not necessarily so. Reason tells us there must be a Being who determined its existence, and this is the necessary Being, whom we call God, the Creator of heaven and earth.

4. Perfection, Relative and Absolute

By the comparative perfection in nature, we can

Sound Reasoning Leads to God

argue to the fact that God is a perfect Being. There is an old Latin adage: "Nemo dat, quod non habet. No one can give what he has not." No cause can convey to its effect what it has not. But he may have the cause of it in a higher and nobler form. To illustrate: there is a beautiful picture painted by an artist. People admire this masterpiece. Not the paint, but the mind of the artist is the efficient cause of that masterpiece. The conception of his mind he put on canvas. The picture represents a Saint. The artist thought of the virtues, of the kindness, of the heroism, and many other noble qualities of a Saint. By this painting the spiritual thought appears in material shape. In a more eminent manner all that is contained in the picture was contained in the idea of the artist. The perfections of the masterpiece reflect the idea and skill of the artist. The artist gave shape and expression to it in the color on the canvas. No one can confer a perfection, which he does not in some way or other possess.

The world is God's creation. There is a great deal of beauty in this world. God who caused it must be beautiful. He must possess beauty in a more eminent degree. There is power in the world. God who caused it must be powerful. There is intelligence in creatures. In the Creator we find it in all its perfection. There is wisdom displayed in the harmony of this world. The Creator thereof must be more eminently wise. The perfections found in the effect argue to the perfections of the cause.

By the comparisons we make of relative value and

perfections in nature, we unconsciously profess our belief in God. Some of the things in this world are better than others. Some are more beautiful than others; some are more powerful, and so on. It is all comparative, showing degrees of perfection. Higher and lower, good and better, more or less are plainly relative terms. That implies that there must be a standard somewhere in relation to which a thing has comparative perfection. A relative perfection without an absolute perfection is rank nonsense; for relative thus used always indicates a comparison with the absolute. That absolute standard of perfection is such that no higher degree of perfection can be possible; it is infinite perfection. Therefore the relative perfections found in this world prove the existence of infinite perfections, which are not found in the creation but must be found and are found in the Creator, in God. God is infinitely perfect. As to duration God is eternal. As to His manifestations God is all-powerful, all-knowing, all-wise, all-just, all-merciful, the Creator and Preserver of every creature.

5. Design

No matter what thing in nature we analyze we find symmetry in its construction. There is symmetry in a snowflake, in a crystal and in all vegetation. In everything we behold construction, the adjustment of parts for the fulfillment of a given purpose. Everything in nature has a specific tendency. We cannot help to observe laws in nature, neither can we refrain from admiring the grand mechanism in the heavenly bodies

Sound Reasoning Leads to God

and in things on earth. That presupposes an Intelligent Adjuster who designed with a purpose; and He is God.

6. Law and Lawgiver

One of the laws of nature is the law of gravitation, whereby all matter tends toward the center of the earth. Water runs downhill no matter what people decree. Supposing the whole world would demand that water run uphill; that demand is futile because the laws of nature are not depending upon man's likes and dislikes. This also includes centrifugal force, etc. Who made this law? Man could not make it. The author of this law we call God. Wherever there is a law, there must be a lawgiver.

7. Conscience

Our conscience tells us that certain things are right, and other things are wrong for us to do. There is a law of right, as well as of truth. Every human being, not deprived of good common sense, knows that there is a natural law of right and wrong. Like all natural laws it is not and was not made by man. The author of all nature is the author of that law. There can be no law without a lawgiver. Our conscience tells us of the law. A little reasoning leads us to the conclusion that there cannot be a law without a lawgiver, and since this law is not made by man, it must be made by some other intelligent personal Being. This Being we call God. Our conscience tells us what we ought to do, what God wants us to do; that we must do good, obey

God's will, and avoid sin, which is a transgression of God's laws. By its praise for the good done, and by its rebuke for the evil, our conscience tells us that God as a just Being demands an account of all our deliberate actions and omissions. As reason tells us that God is the cause and destiny of our existence, so our conscience decides within us whether we are tending to our destiny, or not.

Who Is God?

God is the prime cause of the whole universe and of everything that is in it. God called everything into existence. He set His creation in motion and it is now whirling around or about in space. God is the only Necessary Being on whom all contingent beings depend for their existence and sustenance. He is the absolutely perfect Being as proclaimed by the relative goodness and perfection in creation. God is infinitely perfect and created everything for a specific purpose. There is symmetry and order in His creation. God is our Creator, our First Cause and our Final Destiny. Reason, therefore, tells us that God is our Creator, Preserver, our greatest Benefactor and that we owe Him gratitude for the favors received. We depend on Him utterly. To deny the existence of God is the same as to deny your common sense. It is the same as to go contrary to the conviction upon which your intellect acts under the voice of conscience. Shutting your eyes against the light causes darkness; wilful darkness, as far as you are concerned. Withhold the use of your intellect and you are in the darkness of sin-

Sound Reasoning Leads to God

ful folly. The man who closes his eyes and then complains that he cannot see is acting stupidly. The man who does not reason, and in spite of all evidence does not know anything about God, or even denies God, is justly called a fool. "The fool hath said in his heart: there is no God." Ps. 13:1.

If I observe a piece of paper whereon something is written, I know that an intelligent person has expressed his idea or at least some idea, a thought on matter. Those material letters before me are evidence of an immaterial agency, thought conveyed on matter. When a man walks I know he is alive. I do not see his soul, his life-principle, but I notice its influence on the material body that moves along. His soul is there.

Where Is God?

God's handwriting is everywhere. God is on earth in every place and in everything. The earth is full of creatures. A creature is a manifestation of the Creator. No creature can exist by itself; of necessity it needs the support of the Creator. Ascend in spirit up to the firmament and see the majestic orbs coursing along their designated orbits. God's omnipotence keeps them there. Where there is a display of His present omnipotent work, there is God. Dive down into the depths of the sea and behold the creatures on the bottom of the ocean. Who provides for them and keeps them alive? There is the work of God; God is there. God is everywhere. God is infinite in all His perfections; there can be no limit to His presence. Where is God? God is here. Though you know it not, God is with you in every place. When you sought the lonely place of sin and shame, you were walking in God's presence. God saw you. God sees and observes you this very moment. Where is God? God is visible to the Angels and Saints in Heaven; but He is not only there, He is everywhere. Reason tells us that an infinite self-existent Being cannot be limited.

"O Lord, our Lord, how admirable is thy name in the whole earth." Ps. 8:1.

"But ask now the beasts, and they shall teach thee: and the birds of the air, and they shall tell thee.

"Speak to the earth, and it shall answer thee: and the fishes of the sea shall tell.

"Who is ignorant that the hand of the Lord hath made all these things?

"In whose hand is the soul of every living thing, and the spirit of all flesh of man.

"Doth not the ear discern words, and the palate of him that eateth, the taste?" Job 12:7-11.

"The heavens shew forth the glory of God, and the firmament declareth the work of His hands.

"Day to day uttereth speech, and night to night sheweth knowledge.

"There are no speeches nor languages, where their voices are not heard.

"Their sound hath gone forth into all the earth: and their words to the ends of the world." Ps. 18:1-5.

"For thy magnificence is elevated above the heavens. Out of the mouth of infants and of sucklings thou hast perfected praise, because of thy enemies, that thou mayest destroy the enemy and the avenger.

Sound Reasoning Leads to God

"For I will behold the heavens, the works of thy fingers: the moon and the stars which thou hast founded.

"What is man that thou art mindful of him? or the son of man that thou visitest him?

"Thou hast made him a little less than the angels, thou hast crowned him with glory and honor: and hast set him over the works of thy hands.

"Thou hast subjected all things under his feet, all sheep and oxen: moreover the beasts also of the fields.

"The birds of the air, and the fishes of the sea, that pass through the paths of the sea.

"O Lord, our Lord, how admirable is thy name in all the earth!" Ps. 8:2-10.

Oh what a lesson does that teach us! God sees me. In need I am not entirely forsaken; God is with me.

"But all men are vain, in whom there is not the knowledge of God: and who by these good things that are seen, could not understand him that is, neither by attending to the works have acknowledged who was the workman:

"But have imagined either the fire, or the wind, or the swift air, or the circle of the stars, or the great water, or the sun and moon, to be the gods that rule the world.

"With whose beauty, if they, being delighted, took them to be gods: let them know how much the Lord of them is more beautiful than they: for the first author of beauty made all those things.

"Or if they admired their power and their effects,

let them understand by them, that He that made them is mightier than they:

"For by the greatness of the beauty, and of the creature, the creator of them may be seen, so as to be known thereby." Wis. 13:1-6.

St. Paul brings home a similar lesson when he writes, "For the invisible things of him, from the creation of the world, are clearly seen, being understood by the things that are made; His eternal power also, and divinity: so that they are inexcusable." Rom. 1:20.

Jesus, the Son of God

THE following pages will adduce a few biblical testimonies for the divinity of Jesus Christ.

The belief in the divinity of Jesus Christ is not a mere feeling; it is based upon the fact that God has made this truth known.

God can reveal truths directly or indirectly through His agents. When He speaks through another He supplies this agent of His with the credentials necessary to assure us of the fact that he is God's spokesman. Such credentials are holiness of life and loftiness of doctrine, but especially miracles and prophecies. When a person performs acts that can be performed only by the power of God, or when he foretells with certainty future events that can be known only by the foreknowledge of God, and if he appeals to these miracles and prophecies as the proof of the truth of his mission, we know that he is a spokesman of God.

The prophets in the Old Testament had such credentials. In the New Testament the Apostles had them. When they worked miracles or prophesied they did so by the power and knowledge which God communicated to them. They acted in the name of God. They did not profess to do so in their own name.

There has been one person, however, who worked many miracles and who uttered many prophecies, and did so in His own name. That person is Jesus Christ. By His miracles and prophecies He proved that He was a spokesman of God. Therefore, what He taught must be true. And one of the truths that He taught is the fact that He Himself is the true Son of God.

Jesus performed miracles in His own name. God alone can do this. Therefore His miracles are evidences of His divinity.

We have selected a few of the most telling testimonies of the divinity of Christ in this brochure. May these few pages strengthen you in your faith and give you convenient arguments for the belief in the divinity of Jesus Christ.

Testimony of the Prophets

As a rule, the biography of a person is not written till after his death, seldom during his lifetime, and never before his birth. But wonderful to relate, the entire life-story of Jesus Christ, the Son of the Blessed Virgin Mary, was minutely told hundreds of years before His birth. The Old Testament contains the entire life of Jesus Christ in prophecy. Even the circumstances of His life were told: namely, that He would be born of a Virgin, in Bethlehem, during the time of universal peace, when a star would appear in the East. His flight into Egypt was foretold, His coming into the Temple, sitting among the doctors and instructing them, His hidden life, and in detail, His public life. The prophets in advance described Him as a Good Shepherd, as a doer of wonderful works, as a teacher, as a prophet, and as the Redeemer of the world. His suffering, His agony, His death on the cross, His burial and glorious resurrection, His ascension into Heaven, and the continuity of His Church;

Jesus, the Son of God

these and many more things were foretold of Him and were literally fulfilled in Jesus Christ.

Testimony of St. Elizabeth

When the Blessed Virgin Mary visited Elizabeth, St. John the Baptist was sanctified in his mother's womb. At that moment St. Elizabeth said among other things: "Whence is this to me, that the Mother of my Lord should come to me?" St. Luke 1:43.

Testimony of St. John the Baptist

John saw Jesus coming to him, and he said: "Behold the Lamb of God, behold him who taketh away the sin of the world." St. John 1:29.

Testimony of His Heavenly Father

"And Jesus being baptized, forthwith came out of the water: and lo, the heavens were opened to Him: and he saw the Spirit of God descending as a dove, and coming upon Him. And behold a voice from heaven, saying: *This is My beloved Son, in Whom I am well pleased.*" St. Matt. 3:16, 17.

Testimony of Jesus Christ Himself

Jesus Christ gave ample proof of His Divinity. He showed His unlimited power over the elements of nature. Upon His command the water blushed into wine; loaves of bread were miraculously multiplied, the bouncing waves of the sea served Him for a solid pathway as He walked over them and came to His frightened Apostles, who were struggling against the waves and the storm; He commanded the wind and the waves, and there came a great calm; He cursed the fig tree and it withered. All nature obeyed His commands. Therefore He is the Lord of all nature.

He is supernatural. He cured the sick as He pleased by His simple command. He restored eyesight to the blind, hearing to the deaf, speech to the mute and the use of their limbs to the palsied, feverish, lepers and cripples. He drove out devils and restored the dead to life. Jairus with his wife and friends wept over the death of his young daughter, a girl of twelve years. Jesus took the dead girl by the hand and said: "Talitha cumi, which is, being interpreted: Damsel, (I say to thee) arise. And immediately the damsel rose up, and walked." St. Mark 5:41, 42. At another time, probably previous to this event, we see Jesus at the gate of the city of Naim. "And when He came nigh to the gate of the city, behold a dead man was carried out, the only son of his mother; and she was a widow; and a great multitude of the city was with her. Whom when the Lord had seen, being moved with mercy towards her, He said to her: Weep not, and He came near and touched the bier. And they that carried it, stood still. And He said: Young man, I say to thee, arise. And he that was dead, sat up and began to speak. And He gave him to his mother." St. Luke 7:12, 15. Shortly before His bitter passion Jesus went out to the grave of Lazarus, who had been dead for four days. In the presence of Lazarus' sisters, Martha and Mary, and in the presence of many persons, after the stone had been removed from the sepulchre, Jesus "cried with a loud voice: Lazarus, come forth. And presently he that had been dead came forth, bound feet and hands with the winding bands, and his face was bound about with a napkin. Jesus said to them: Loose him, and let him go. Many therefore of the Jews, who were come to Mary and Martha, and had seen the things that Jesus did, believed in Him." St. John 11:43-45. Thus Jesus repeatedly gave proof of His omnipotence. He proved His omniscience by the many contingent things which He foretold and which have been fulfilled. We shall mention only some of them: the betrayal of Himself by Judas; His own bitter passion and bloody death; His glorious resurrection; His ascension; and the persecution and perpetuity of His Church.

When St. Peter said: "Thou art Christ, the Son of the living God, Jesus answering, said to him: Blessed art thou, Simon Bar-Jona: because flesh and blood hath not revealed it to thee, but My Father Who is in Heaven." St. Matt. 16:16, 17. When the Jewish high priest had said: "I adjure thee by the living God, that thou tell us if thou be the Christ, the Son of God, Jesus saith to him: Thou hast said it. Nevertheless I say to you, hereafter you shall see the Son of man sitting on the right hand of the power of God, and coming in the clouds of heaven." St. Matt. 26: 63, 64. "But hereafter the Son of man shall be sitting on the right hand of the power of God. Then said they all: Art thou then the Son of God? Who said: You say that I am." St. Luke 22:69, 70. "For God so loved the world, as to give His only begotten Son; that whosoever believeth in Him, may not perish, but may have life everlasting." St. John 3:16.

However the most convincing proof of His divinity,

to which He Himself so often referred, is His glorious resurrection. Great is the skill and the power of man. But no man has either skill or power over his own body after the soul leaves it in death. From that moment on the body remains helpless. There is only one exception to this. Jesus had promised that He would rise from the dead on the third day after His crucifixion. His heart had been pierced and slashed with a lance and the last drop of His Precious Blood oozed forth. Soldiers guarded His grave. The third day began to dawn and Jesus came forth alive from the grave and appeared to His Apostles and disciples for forty days. They all saw Him and they frequently spoke to Him and many of them saw Him ascend into Heaven. In testimony of His Godhead the Apostles and many others at their time and since that time have performed astounding miracles in the name of Jesus. Jesus is God. May He be loved and faithfully adored by all of us until a happy death brings us into His visible presence.

Testimony of Evangelists and Apostles

"And when they were come up into the boat, the wind ceased. And they that were in the boat came and adored him, saying: Indeed thou art the Son of God." St. Matt. 14:32, 33.

Testimony of St. Mark

"The beginning of the gospel of Jesus Christ, the Son of God." St. Mark 1:1.

Testimony of St. John

"And the Word was made flesh, and dwelt among

Jesus, the Son of God

us, (and we saw his glory, the glory as it were of the only begotten of the Father,) full of grace and truth." St. John 1:14.

"Many other signs also did Jesus in the sight of his disciples, which are not written in this book. But these are written, that you may believe that Jesus is the Christ, the Son of God: and that believing, you may have life in his name." St. John 20:30, 31.

Testimony of St. Peter

"Simon Peter answered and said: Thou art Christ, the Son of the living God." St. Matt. 16:16. "Then Jesus said to the twelve: Will you also go away? And Simon Peter answered Him: Lord, to whom shall we go? Thou hast the words of eternal life. And we have believed and have known, that Thou art the Christ, the Son of God." St. John 6:68-70.

Testimony of St. Paul

"Who is the image of the invisible God, the firstborn of every creature:

"For in him were all things created in heaven and on earth, visible and invisible, whether thrones, or dominations, or principalities, or powers: all things were created by him and in him.

"And he is before all, and by him all things consist.

"And he is the head of the body, the church, who is the beginning, the firstborn from the dead; that in all things he may hold the primacy." Col. 1:15-18.

"For let this mind be in you, which was also in Christ Jesus: "Who being in the form of God, thought it not robbery to be equal with God." Phil. 2:5, 6.

"God, who, at sundry times and in divers manners, spoke in times past to the fathers by the prophets, last of all, "In these days hath spoken to us by his Son, whom he hath appointed heir of all things, by whom also he made the world. Who being the brightness of his glory, and the figure of his substance, and upholding all things by the word of his power, making purgation of sins, sitteth on the right hand of the majesty on high." Heb. 1:1-3.

Testimony of the Centurion

"Now the centurion and they that were with him watching Jesus, having seen the earthquake and the things that were done, were sore afraid, saying: Indeed this was the Son of God." St. Matt. 27:54.

Testimony of Flavius Josephus, born 36, died 96 A.D.

In his 18th Book of the Antiquities of the Jews, Chapter III, No. 3, he writes: "Now, there was about this time Jesus, a wise man, if it be lawful to call Him a man, for He was a doer of wonderful works, a teacher of such men as receive the truth with pleasure. He drew over to Him both many of the Jews and many of the Gentiles. He was (the) Christ: and when Pilate, at the suggestion of the principal men among us, had condemned Him to the cross, those that loved Him at the first did not forsake Him, for He appeared to them alive again the third day, as the divine prophets had foretold these and the thousand other wonderful things concerning Him; and the tribe of christians, so named for Him, are not extinct at this day."

The Catholic Church

Jesus Christ Is the Founder of the Catholic Church

JESUS CHRIST is the founder of the Catholic Church. It is the only Church that dates back to Him. Every other Christian denomination has a human origin and is of a more recent date.

Jesus Christ is the Son of God. Hundreds of years before He was born of the Blessed Virgin Mary at Bethlehem and so many centuries before the angels of Heaven and a wonderful star in the east announced His advent, the divinely inspired prophets of old minutely foretold the signs of the times, the circumstances of His birth and the entire life-story of Jesus Christ.

His flight into Egypt and His return to Nazareth, His coming into the Temple are incidents of the rather hidden life which He spent in the company of the Blessed Virgin and St. Joseph, his foster father. At the age of thirty years Jesus entered upon His public life. He went about preaching the gospel of salvation and doing good. Every now and then He gave a proof of His omnipotence by performing miracles in His own name. The elements of nature obeyed His voice, and thus He showed that His power is supernatural. He calmed the storm on the sea. He changed water into wine by His omnipotent will. Twice He multiplied loaves of bread miraculously. He healed all kinds of disease without medicine. The bouncing waves of the sea served Him as a solid pathway as He walked over them and hastened to His frightened disciples and said: "It is I; be not afraid." St. John 6:20.

He spoke with divine authority as He pointed out the way of salvation. Even His enemies declared: "Never did man speak like this man." St. John 7:46. "The people were in admiration of his doctrine. For he was teaching them as one having power, and not as the scribes and Pharisees." St. Matt. 7:28, 29.

Jesus drove out evil spirits. "And devils went out from many, crying out and saying: Thou art the Son of God. And rebuking them he suffered them not to speak, for they knew that he was Christ." St. Luke 4:41.

"And having called his twelve disciples together, he gave them power over unclean spirits to cast them out and to heal all manner of diseases, and all manner of infirmities. And the names of the twelve apostles are these: The first, Simon who is called Peter, and Andrew his brother, James the son of Zebedee, and John his brother, Philip and Bartholomew, Thomas and Matthew the publican, and James the son of Alpheus, and Thaddeus, Simon the Cananean, and Judas Iscariot, who also betrayed him." St. Matt. 10:1-4.

These twelve Apostles Jesus sent out to preach His gospel and to help in saving souls. He appointed St. Peter as the visible head of the whole Church. When St. Peter made a public profession of his faith and said to Jesus: "Thou art Christ, the Son of the living God," Jesus said to him: "Blessed art thou, Simon Bar-Jona: because flesh and blood hath not revealed it to thee, but my Father who is in heaven. And I say to thee: That thou art Peter; and upon this rock I will build my church, and the gates of hell shall not prevail against it. And I will give to thee the keys of the kingdom of heaven. And whatsoever thou shalt bind upon earth, it shall be bound also in heaven: and whatsoever thou shalt loose on earth, it shall be loosed also in heaven." St. Matt. 16:16-19.

At the sea of Tiberias in the presence of Thomas, Nathaniel, John and James, Jesus said to Simon Peter: "Simon, son of John, lovest thou me more than these? He saith to him: Yea, Lord, thou knowest that I love thee. He saith to him: Feed my lambs. He saith to him again: Simon, son of John, lovest thou me? He saith to him: Yea, Lord, thou knowest that I love thee. He saith to him: Feed my lambs. He said to him the third time: Simon, son of John, lovest thou me? Peter was grieved, because he had said to him the third time: Lovest thou me? And he said to him: Lord, thou knowest all things: thou knowest that I love thee. He said to him: Feed my sheep." St. John 21:15-17. Lambs and sheep constitute the entire flock. Jesus loved to call Himself the Good Shepherd. St. Peter was to feed His flock; that is to say, St. Peter was appointed by Him as the supreme visible head of the Church.

Jesus founded but one Church. He called it the kingdom of Heaven, and likened it to a vineyard, to a grain of mustard-seed, to a garden, to a field, to a sheepfold, to a flock, to a net, to a banquet, to a house built on a mountain. All these figures, as well as His direct words to St. Peter, indicate that His Church is one. He founded but one Church for the salvation of all mankind. As a matter of fact, every reader of the holy Bible knows that Christ established but one Church. After Jesus Christ had labored and preached and manifested His divinity by miracles, He was sentenced to death on account of His assertion: "I am the Son of God." St. Matt. 27:43. He died for the redemption of the world. As He had repeatedly foretold, He by His own omnipotence rose on the third day from the dead. By His glorious resurrection He gave to the world a convincing proof that He is God. For forty days after His resurrection He appeared to His disciples and spoke to them of the kingdom of God, of the coming of the Holy Ghost, of the primacy of St. Peter, and of many other important things.

Shortly before His ascension into heaven Jesus said to them: "All power is given to me in heaven and in earth. Going therefore, teach ye all nations; baptizing them in the name of the Father, and of the Son, and of the Holy Ghost. Teaching them to observe all things whatsoever I have commanded you: and behold I am with you all days, even to the consummation of the world." St. Matt. 28:18-20.

Jesus is with His Church all days, even to the consummation of the world. Hence His Church must last to the end of the world. It must continue throughout all centuries. If so, then His Church is still in existence. And so it is. History bears witness to the fact, that the Church which Jesus founded is still extant. The Church which Jesus founded is the only divine Church; it is the only one which can save mankind. His Church is God-made, all other churches are man-made. They are human in origin and in effect. All who earnestly desire to be saved must belong to the Church which Jesus Christ instituted and of which He plainly said: "The gates of hell shall not prevail against it."

It will not do to say that the Church of which the Apostles were the first bishops and teachers *was* the true Church; no, that Church *continues* to be the only true Church. Jesus remains with it. "Behold I am with you all days, even to the consummation of the world." Neither may any person belonging to a rather new religion imagine that his church can save him, because it bears some resemblance to the Church which Jesus founded more than 1900 years ago. No, the saving Church is not only *like* it, but it is *identical* with the Church of which Jesus Christ is the founder. God established only one Church for the salvation of mankind. In that Church all the necessary means of salvation are deposited. Whosoever refuses to be a loyal member of the true Church and thus deliberately deprives himself of the means of salvation will be lost. "He said to them: Go ye into the whole world, and preach the gospel to every creature. He that believeth and is baptized, shall be saved: but he that believeth not shall be condemned." St. Mark 16: 15, 16.

That is the true Church of which the incarnate Son of God is the founder, which bears the undeniable mark of historic continuity. It is the same Church with the same unalterable doctrines, the same necessary and helpful means of grace, the same divine sacraments, the same holy sacrifice and everything the same which Jesus Christ ordained as necessary for salvation. The visible head of that Church must be the legitimate successor of St. Peter, vested with the same authority to feed the whole flock of Christ. Above all, the true Church must date back to Christ. Any church which is of a later date, is not the Church which Jesus founded, not the one which is to continue all days to the end of time. A *purely natural* organization, started by man, can never produce *supernatural* results. In matters of religion it will not do simply to follow the fashion, as so many people seem to think. There is only one saving Church. This is the Church which Jesus Christ founded more than 1900 years ago. "If he will not hear the church, let him be to thee as the heathen and publican." St. Matt. 18:17. "There are some that trouble you, and would pervert the gospel of Christ. But though we, or an angel from heaven, preach a gospel to you besides that which we have preached to you, let him be anathema. As we said before, so now I say again: If anyone preach to you a gospel, besides that which you have received, let him be anathema. For do I now persuade men, or God? Or do I seek to please men? If I yet pleased men, I should not be the servant of Christ. For I give you to understand, brethren, that the gospel which was preached by me is not according to man. For neither did I receive it of man, nor did I learn it; but by the revelation of Jesus Christ." Gal. 1:7-12. St. Paul, therefore, strictly forbids any change of the gospel which he preached. No man, not even an angel, has a right to alter the gospel of Christ. That gospel was preached by all the Apostles long before the New Testament was written. It included a great deal more than the fragmentary narratives contained in the New Testament. At the end of his gospel, St. John expressly says: "But there are also many other things which Jesus did; which, if they were written every one, the world itself, I think, would not be able to contain the books that should be written." St. John 21:25. St. Paul admonishes the Thessalonians: "Therefore, brethren, stand fast; and hold the traditions which you have learned whether by word, or by our epistle." 2 Thess. 2:14. "Hold the form of sound words, which thou hast heard of me in faith, and in the love which is in Christ Jesus. Keep the good thing committed to thy trust by the Holy Ghost, who dwelleth in us." 2 Tim. 1:13, 14.

Really, I do not understand under what pretense of logic or revelation any man of education can assert that the Bible is the sole rule of faith, and that reason, private opinion, is the sole interpreter. St. Paul emphasizes the necessity to *stand fast* and *to hold the traditions,* not to listen to another gospel, not to be tossed to and fro, and carried about with every wind of doctrine. "This then I say and testify in the Lord. that henceforward you walk not as also the gentiles walk in the vanity of their mind." Eph. 4:17.

The true Church positively teaches with divine authority what we must believe and do in order to be saved. Our private opinion must be in conformity with the tenets of the infallible Church. It would be the height of arrogance to presume that God's teachings and means of salvation should depend upon their being accepted or rejected by a poor sinner. God teaches; we must believe. He commands; we must obey. He points out the way of salvation; we must follow His directions.

The authority to teach and to command Jesus Christ lodged with the Apostles and their rightful successors in office. Our duty it is to believe and to obey. This is the ordinance or rule of faith established by God. No person, not even an angel from heaven, has the right to interpret Holy Scripture in any sense different from the teaching authority of the Church.

Any denomination maintaining that the Bible is the sole rule of faith and conceding to every fallible person the right to interpret the written revelations as he pleases, is essentially different from the Church which Jesus Christ founded and of which St. Paul was one of the Apostles.

"Grace be unto you and peace from him that is, and that was, and that is to come, and from the seven spirits which are before his throne. And from JESUS CHRIST, who is the faithful witness, the first begotten of the dead, and the prince of the kings of the earth, who hath loved us, and washed us from our sins in his own blood, and hath made us a kingdom,

The Catholic Church

and priests to God and his Father, to him be glory and empire for ever and ever. Amen." Apoc. 1:4-6.

QUESTIONS ON THE TEXT

1. Who is the founder of the Catholic Church?
2. To whom does it date back?
3. Who is Jesus Christ?
4. What did the Prophets foretell of Him?
5. Mention some of His miracles.
6. What power did Jesus confer upon His Apostles soon after their appointment?
7. What did His enemies declare?
8. How was St. Peter appointed head of the Church?
9. How do you prove that Jesus founded one Church only?
10. Will the Church last till the end of time?
11. Substantiate the historic continuity of the Church.
12. Is the Bible the sole rule of faith? Give reasons for your answer.
13. Has the Church human or divine authority to teach?

TESTIMONY OF WELL-KNOWN WRITERS OF THE FIRST FIVE CENTURIES

From the numerous writings of the early Fathers of the Church and other ecclesiastical writers who lived many centuries ago, but whose writings are still extant, we can easily cull unimpeachable testimony of the fact that the Catholic Church with its Pope at Rome is the same Church which Jesus Christ established for the salvation of immortal souls, and that every true Christian must obey this Church. For brevity's sake I cite only a few of the many able writers of the first five centuries of the Christian era.

St. Clement ✠ 100.

St. Clement, whom St. Paul (Phil. 4:3) calls his fellow laborer, was according to St. Irenaeus the third successor of St. Peter (Peter, Linus, Anacletus, Clement). Tertullian informs us that St. Clement was ordained by St. Peter, the Apostle. History tells us that he was Bishop of Rome whilst St. John was still Bishop of Ephesus. The authenticity of St. Clement's first letter to the Corinthians cannot be called in question. This letter, or Epistle, as it is generally called, was written a few years before his death, which occurred about the year 100 after Christ. Pope St. Clement writes:

"The Apostles have preached to us the Gospel (which they had received) from the Lord Jesus Christ: Jesus Christ from God. Christ, therefore, was sent by God, and the Apostles by Christ. . . . While preaching, therefore, in country places and cities, they appointed their first fruits—having proved them by the Spirit—bishops and deacons of those who were about to believe." No. 42. "So also our Apostles knew, through the Lord Jesus Christ, that contention would arise on account of the episcopal dignity. For this reason, therefore, having a perfect knowledge, they appointed the aforesaid (bishops and deacons) and then gave a rule for future succession, so that when these should die, other approved men might take over their ministry and office." No. 44. "It is shameful, my beloved, it is most shameful, and unworthy of a Christian conduct, that it should be heard that the most firm and ancient church of the Corinthians, on account of one or two persons, is in a sedition against the priests." No. 47.

"Do ye, therefore, who laid the foundation of this sedition, submit to the priests, and accept a punishment unto repentance, bending the knees of your hearts! Learn to be subject, laying aside all proud and arrogant boasting of your tongues; for it is better for you to be found in the fold of Christ, than, thinking yourselves above others, to be cast out of its hope." No. 57.

St. Ignatius ✢ 107.

St. Ignatius was a disciple of St. John, the Apostle and Evangelist, and became the third bishop of Antioch, St. Peter being the first. St. Ignatius succeeded Evodius in the episcopal see of that city, and governed the diocese down to the reign of Emperor Trajan. On his way to Rome (where he suffered martyrdom in the amphitheatre in 107), he wrote seven Epistles, namely: one each to the Ephesians, Magnesians, Trallians, Romans, Philadelphians, to the people of Smyrna, and to their bishop, his dear friend St. Polycarp.

These letters are gems of Christian literature.

In his Epistle to the Ephesians St. Ignatius writes: "It becomes you to concur in the mind of your bishop, as you really do. For your praiseworthy priesthood, worthy of God, is so aptly adjusted to the bishop as strings to a harp. . . . Let no man deceive himself; if a man be not within the altar, he stands deprived of the Bread of God. . . . Whomsoever the Master of the house sendeth to govern His household, we ought to so receive, as we would receive Him that sent him. It is plain, then, that we must receive the bishop as the Lord Himself. Obey the bishop and the priests with an undivided mind, breaking one Bread, which is the medicine of immortality, an antidote that we may not die, but live for ever in Jesus Christ." No. 4, 5, 6, and 20.

"Be ye careful to do all things in divine concord. This, because the bishop presides in the place of God, and the priests are as the senate of the Apostles and the deacons have confided to them the ministry of Jesus Christ." No. 6. "As therefore our Lord, being united with the Father, did nothing without Him, neither by Himself, nor by His Apostles, so neither do you do anything apart from the bishop and the priests. . . . There is one Jesus Christ, than whom nothing is better. Wherefore, hasten ye all together as unto one temple of God; as unto one altar, as unto one Jesus Christ." Epistle to the Magnesians, No. 7.

To the Trallians St. Ignatius wrote: "Let all reverence the deacons as Jesus Christ, and also the bishop; for he is the image of the Father, but the priests as the senate of God and the college of the Apostles. *Without these one cannot speak of the Church.*" Trall. 3, 1. "Protect yourselves, therefore, against such as these men (heretics); and this you will do, if you are not puffed up, nor separated from the God Jesus Christ, and from the bishop, and from the regulations of the Apostles. He that is within the altar is clean; but he that is without, is not; that is, he that does aught without the bishop, the priests, and the deacons; he is not clean in conscience." Epistle to the Trallians, No. 7.

"Love unity; avoid divisions; be ye followers of Jesus Christ, even as He is of the Father." Epistle to the Philadelphians, No. 7. "I cried out with a loud voice, with the voice of God: hold fast to the bishop, to the priests, and to the deacons," Philadelphians, 7:1.

"May you all follow the bishop even as Jesus Christ follows the Father. . . . Where the bishop appears, there let the multitude be also; *even as where Christ is, there is the Catholic Church.*" Epistle to the People of Smyrna, No. 8.

In fact, almost every paragraph of the Ignatian letters emphasizes this unity of the Catholic Church under its divinely instituted tripartite hierarchy as absolutely necessary.

St. Polycarp ✣ 155.

St. Polycarp was instructed by the Apostle St. John. His own disciple, St. Irenaeus, says: "Polycarp was not only taught by the Apostles, and had held intercourse with those who had seen Christ, but was also appointed by the Apostles as bishop over the church of Smyrna in Asia; he likewise always taught this which he had learned from the Apostles, and which he also handed down to the Church, and which alone is true." Against Heresies, Bk. 3, Chap. 3, No. 4.

About the middle of the second century St. Polycarp went to Rome to consult with Pope Anicetus in order to bring about the desired uniformity as to the day of celebrating Easter. When Statius Quadratus the Proconsul tried to persuade him to renounce Jesus Christ, St. Polycarp answered: "Eighty-six years have I served Him, and He never did me any wrong; how then can I blaspheme my King, who redeemed me?" Encyclical Letter of the Church of Smyrna, No. 9. Pierced with a dagger St. Polycarp died for his faith, Feb. 23, 155. To the Philippians, No. 5, he gave this admonition: "Wherefore it is necessary to abstain from all these things, being subject to the presbyters (priests) and deacons as unto God and Christ."

St. Justin ✢ 167.

St. Justin, the philosopher, is the most renowned apologetic writer of the second century. He died a martyr's death about the year 167. In his dialogue with the Jew Trypho, No. 63, St. Justin writes: "Likewise these words (Ps. 94:7-13) plainly prove that because those who believe in Him are one soul and one synagogue and one Church, therefore this Church is addressed by the divine writings as a daughter, being established after His name and sharing the same; for we are all called Christians."

Commenting on Malachias, chapter 1, verse 10, St. Justin writes in the same work: "Not even now is your race *from the rising to the setting of the sun*, but there are nations in which not even one of your nation has ever dwelt. But there is no race of men,—whether of barbarians or of Greeks, or, in fine, bearing any other name because they live in wagons, or are without a fixed home, or dwell in tents leading a pastoral life—among whom prayers and eucharists are not offered to the Father and Creator of the universe through the name of the crucified Jesus." No. 117.

ST. IRENAEUS ✠ 202.

St. Irenaeus, a disciple of St. Polycarp, was ordained priest by Pothinus, Bishop and Martyr, whom he also succeeded as bishop of Lyons. He suffered martyrdom about the year 202.

"For the Church, though spread over the whole world to the earth's boundaries, having received from the Apostles and their disciples the faith in one God, the Father Almighty . . . and in one Christ Jesus, the Son of God made flesh for our salvation, and in the Holy Spirit . . . having received this gospel and this faith, as stated before, the Church, though spread over the whole world, preserves it with the greatest diligence and care as if dwelling in *one* house; and these truths she uniformly holds, as having one soul, and one and the same heart; and these she proclaims and teaches, and hands down uniformly, as though she had but one mouth. For although the world's languages are various, still the force of tradition is one and the same. And neither do the churches founded in Germany believe or deliver a different faith, not those in Spain, in Gaul, in the East, in Egypt, in Africa, or in the regions in the middle of the earth (i. e., Palestine and Jerusalem); but as God's handiwork, the sun, is one and the same throughout the universe, so the preaching of the truth shines everywhere and enlightens all men that wish to come to the knowledge of the truth. Nor does he who, amongst the bishops of the churches, is more powerful in word, deliver a different doctrine from the above (for no one is above his teacher); nor does he who is weak in speech weaken the tradition. For the faith being one and the same, it is neither increased by him who has ability to say much concerning it, nor decreased by him who can say but little. . . . The whole Church has one and the same faith throughout the whole world, as we stated above." Against Heresies, Bk. 1, Chap. 10, No. 1, 2, 3.

"Pointing out that *tradition* which the greatest and most ancient and universally known Church,—founded and constituted at Rome by the two most glorious Apostles, Peter and Paul,—derives from the Apostles, and that faith announced to all men, which, through the succession of her bishops has come down to us, we confound all those who, in any way, whether through pleasing themselves, or vain glory, or blindness, and perverse opinion, assemble otherwise than as behooves them. With this church, because of its higher rank, every church must agree, that is, the faithful of all places in which the apostolic tradition has been always preserved by the faithful of all places. The blessed Apostles, therefore, having founded and built up that Church, committed the office of the episcopacy to Linus. Of this Linus, Paul makes mention in his Epistle to Timothy. But he was succeeded by Anacletus, and after him, in the third place from

The Catholic Church

the Apostles, Clement obtains that episcopate,—who had even seen the blessed Apostles themselves, and conferred with them, and who had yet before his eyes the familiar preaching, and the tradition of the Apostles; and not he alone, for there were at that time many alive who had been instructed by the Apostles. . . . But this Clement was succeeded by Evaristus, and Evaristus by Alexander. Next to him, thus the sixth from the Apostles, Sixtus was appointed; and after him Telesphorus, who also suffered a glorious martyrdom; next Hyginus; then Pius; after whom was Anicetus. And since Anicetus was succeeded by Soter, Eleutherus as the twelfth after the Apostles now holds the episcopate. In this order, and by this succession, the tradition which is in the Church from the Apostles, and their preaching of the truth, have come down to us." Against Heresis, Bk. 3, Chap. 3, No. 2, 3.

Origen ✝ 255.

Origen, one of the most prolific writers that ever lived, of whom Epiphanius (Heresis, 64) asserts that he wrote six thousand books, and concerning whom Eusebius tells us that he kept busy seven amanuenses (copyists) by his dictations, was a man of genuine piety. He died at Tyre in 254 or 255 at the age of seventy in consequence of many tortures he underwent while in prison for his faith. Being a man of wonderful endurance, he has received the soubriquet Adamantius. He writes: "For just as we, after we have come to believe that Christ is the Son of God, and that we must learn the truth from Him, have ceased to seek it amongst all those that claimed it with false opinions, seeing that many amongst the Greeks and Barbarians promised it; so since there are many who fancy that they think the things that are of Christ, and yet some of these differ with those that were before them, let the ecclesiastical teaching be preserved, which has been handed down from the Apostles by the order of succession, and which remains in the churches even to this day. That alone is to be believed as the truth, which in nothing differs from the ecclesiastical and apostolic tradition." On the Principles, Introduction, No. 2.

Speaking of St. Peter, Origen exclaims: "Behold, what is said by the Lord to that great foundation of the Church, that most solid rock, upon which Christ founded His Church." Homily 5 on Exodus.

Tertullian ✝ 240.

Tertullian, a Priest at Carthage (died about 240), is highly esteemed by all students of patrology for the originality and individuality of his writings. His rigoristic views on all questions pertaining to morality led him in later years into the sect of the Montanists. His numerous works contain a rich store of information. He knew how to handle the most difficult questions of dogmatic and moral theology in a concise manner.

"It is not lawful for us to introduce anything of our own choice, or even to choose that which any one may have introduced of his own choice. We have as our

The Catholic Church

authorities the Apostles of the Lord, who did not even themselves choose anything by their own will that they might introduce it, but faithfully delivered over to the nations the doctrine which they had received from Christ." On Prescription Against the Heretics, Chapt. 6.

"In short, if it is certain that that is truest which is most ancient, that most ancient which is even from the beginning, that from the beginning which is from the Apostles; it will in like manner also be certain, that that has been handed down by the Apostles, which has been held sacred by the Apostolic Churches. Let us see what milk the Corinthians have received from Paul; . . . what the Philippians, the Thessalonians, the Ephesians read; also what the Romans close at hand trumpet forth, to whom both Peter and Paul left the Gospel sealed even with their blood. We have also the churches taught by John. For although Marcion rejects his Apocalypse, nevertheless the succescion of bishops, counted up to their own origin, will stand by John as the author." Against Marcion, Bk. 4, Chap. 5.

"But if any heretics dare to intrude on the apostolic age, that thus they may seem to have been handed down from the Apostles, we are able to say: Let them, then, make known the origin of their churches; let them unroll the series of their bishops, so coming down by succession from the beginning that their first bishop had for his authority and for his predecessor some one of the Apostles, or of the apostolic men, so he were one that continued steadfast with the

Apostles. For in this manner do the apostolic churches indicate their origins; as the church of Smyrna shows that Polycarp was placed there by John; as that of the Romans adduces Clement, ordained by Peter; similarly, of course, the other churches show those, whom, having been appointed by the Apostles to the episcopate, they have, as transmitters of the apostolic seed." On Prescription Against the Heretics, Ch. 32.

St. Cyprian ✝ 258.

St. Cyprian, who in 248 was consecrated Bishop of Carthage, his native city, wrote several treatises on religious topics and some sixty-five letters mostly dealing with the theological questions of his day. He gained the crown of martyrdom as one of the most glorious Bishops of the *Catholic Church,* Sept. 14th, 258. St. Augustine (On Baptism, III, 3, 5) calls him "Catholic bishop and Catholic martyr." St. Jerome, when passing a criticism on the writings of St. Cyprian (Letter 58, 10) says: "They run like the sweet and placid waters of a pure fountain."

Of the heretic Novation, St. Cyprian remarks in his 52nd letter to Antonianus (No. 24): "That man, notwithstanding God's tradition, notwithstanding the unity of the *Catholic Church* everywhere compacted and conjoined, strives to make a human church, and sends his new apostles through divers cities, in order to lay certain new foundations of his own institution; and though there have long since been ordained, throughout all the provinces and in each city, bishops, men advanced in age, sound in faith, tried in difficul-

ties, proscribed during the persecution, he dares to create other false bishops over them, as if he would traverse the whole world in the obstinacy of his new attempt, or tear asunder the linked union of the ecclesiastical body by scattering the seeds of his discord; forgetful of the fact that schismatics always burn with zeal at the outset, but that that which they have begun unlawfully cannot have increase or growth, but at once begins to languish together with evil jealousy."
... "Since we have these numerous and weighty examples together with many others, whereby God has condescended to confirm the sacerdotal authority and power, what kind of men, thinkest thou, are they, who as enemies of the priesthood, and rebels against the Catholic Church, are not intimidated either by the Lord's forewarning threats, or by the vengeance of a future judgment? For neither have heresies sprung up, nor schisms been engendered from other source; but because the priest of God is not obeyed nor attention given to this, that there is but one priest at a time in the church, and who for the time is judge in Christ's stead; if the whole brotherhood would, according to divine instructions, obey him, no one would agitate in opposition to the college of priests, etc." Letter 55 to Cornelius, No. 5. "Or is perhaps the dignity of the Catholic Church, and the faithful and uncorrupted majesty of the people within her, and even the priestly authority and power, to be set aside to such an extent that men who are set *without* the Church may tell us they wish to judge a prelate of the Church? heretics pass judgment on a Christian?" Ibid. No. 18.

"*He can no longer have God for his father, who has not the Church for his mother.* If any one was able to save himself who was without the ark of Noah, then may he be saved who is outside, out of the Church. The Lord warns and says, *He that is not with me is against me, and he that gathereth not with me, scattereth.* He who rends asunder the peace and concord of Christ's Church, rebels against Christ. He who gathers elsewhere, outside the Church, scatters the Church of Christ. The Lord says, *I and the Father are one;* and again, of the Father, and the Son, and Holy Ghost, it is written, *And these three are one.* And does any one believe that this unity, proceeding from the divine stability and coherent in heavenly mysteries (i. e., the *unity* of the Trinity as just shown) can be rent asunder in the Church, and be split by the dissent of conflicting opinions? He who holds not this unity, holds not the law of God, holds not the faith of the Father and the Son, holds not life and salvation." On the Unity of the Cath. Church, No. 6.

"For although we are many shepherds, yet do we feed but one flock; and we must gather and cherish all the sheep which Christ has purchased with His Blood and His Passion." Letter 67 (to Pope St. Stephen), No. 4.

LACTANTIUS ✝ 330.

Lactantius, the "Christian Cicero," was for some time during his later years the tutor of the unfortunate Crispus, the son of the Emperor Constantine; this classic writer died probably at Trier about 330.

Like Origen, Tertullian and Cyprian, he was a native African. He tells us: "The *Catholic Church* therefore is the only one that retains the true worship. This is the source of truth; this the dwelling-place of faith; this the temple of God; whosoever does not enter this temple, or whosoever departs from it, stands a stranger to the hope of life and eternal salvation." Divine Institutions, Bk. 4, Ch. 30.

EUSEBIUS ✠ 340.

Eusebius, Bishop of Caesarea (died about 340) is called "The Father of Church History." He wrote an extremely valuable work in ten books on the history of the Church from its foundation by Christ down to the year 323. Speaking of Simon Magus, he writes: "But his success was not lasting. For at the same time, while Claudius was still reigning, the all-good and all-benevolent Divine Providence led to Rome the mightiest and the greatest amongst the Apostles: him, who because of his virtues was the spokesman for all the others, Peter namely (to contend) against that mighty destroyer of Life. Armed with divine weapons, he (St. Peter) as God's valiant general, brought the precious merchandise of intellectual light from the East to the dwellers in the West." Ecclesiastical History, Bk. 2; Ch. 14.

"After the martyrdom of Paul and Peter, Linus was chosen in the first place as Bishop of the Roman Church." Eccl. History, Bk. 3; Ch. 2. "He established over the whole earth His city, I mean His Catholic Church, and the assembly of pious men; of which city it is elsewhere said: *Glorious things are said of thee, O city of God.* And, *The stream of the river maketh the city of God joyful.* When, therefore, the prophet desired to behold this *fortified city,* he said, *Who will bring me into the fortified city?* or, *into the city fenced around,* for thus Symmachus translates; for the gates and doors and bolts of the divine powers fence it round, that it may not be oppressed by a siege. Therefore did the Savior say concerning it, *I will build my church upon a rock, and the gates of hell shall not prevail against it.*" Commentary on Ps. 59.

"For the inventions of the enemies soon disappeared being refuted by the truth itself; because while sect after sect appeared with their innovations, the earlier ones always passed away, and splitting up into numerous and manifold forms would go to ruin in one way or another, the only true, the glorious, the Catholic Church, on the contrary, remaining ever firm and ever the self-same in all things, still went on increasing and developing; and showed forth in brilliant light the venerableness, the genuineness, and the nobility, as also the reasonableness and the purity of its divine doctrine and mode of life." Eccl. Hist., Bk. 4, Ch. 11.

St. Athanasius ✣ 373.

St. Athanasius, Patriarch of Alexandria, justly styled the Father of Orthodoxy and surnamed the Great, was a man of a very amiable disposition. We are told that he knew by heart nearly the entire Holy

Bible. Through the envy and hatred of the Arians he was sent into exile five times, but his return was always an occasion of great joy to the faithful. He died as Patriarch of Alexandria, May 2, 373. He is the author of many works, apologetic, dogmatico-polemical, historico-polemical, exegetical, moral, and ascetical. His literary works are deep and clear, combining simplicity of expression with sublimity of thought.

In his first letter to Serapion (No. 28) we read: "But it will hardly be out of place to investigate likewise the ancient tradition, and the doctrine and faith of the Catholic Church, which the Lord communicated, the Apostles proclaimed, and the Fathers preserved; for on this has the Church been founded, and if one falls away from this, he can by no means be a Christian or even be called such any longer."

"The synod of Nicea was not held without reason, but it was brought about because of an urgent need, and for legitimate cause. . . . Respecting Easter they wrote indeed, *It has been decreed as follows*, for it was then decreed that all should obey; but as regards faith, they said by no means, 'It has been decreed,' but *Thus believes the Catholic Church*, and at once confessed *what* they believed, in order to show that their sentiment was not novel, but apostolic. And the things which they handed down in writing were not invented by themselves, but they are the same things which the Apostles have taught." On the Synods, No. 5.

St. Hilary of Poitiers ✣ 366.

St. Hilary of Poitiers was, like many others, converted from heathenism to Christianity by the perusal of Holy Scripture. He wrote a voluminous work in twelve books on the Blessed Trinity, several historico-polemical, a number of biblical commentaries and a few beautiful liturgical hymns. He died as Bishop of Poitiers, Jan. 13, 366.

"In sooth Peter's confession obtained a worthy recompense. Blessed is he that is praised as having directed his thoughts and seen beyond the ken of human eyes, not regarding what was of flesh and blood, but recognizing by revelation the Son of God; as being accounted worthy to be the first to acknowledge what was in the Christ of God. Oh, happy foundation of the Church,—being called by a new name—and a rock worthy of building up of that which was to destroy the infernal laws and the gates of hell, and all the bars of death. O blessed keeper of the gate of heaven, to whose authority are delivered the keys of the eternal portals; whose judgment on earth is an authority prejudged in heaven, so that the things that are either loosed or bound on earth may acquire in heaven a like state of settlement." Commentary on Matt. XVI., No. 7.

"Assuredly, thy kindness must listen to the voice of those who exclaim, 'I am a Catholic, I will not be a heretic; I am a Christian, not an Arian, and better were it for me to suffer death in this world, than to violate the spotless virginity of truth, because of the domineering power of any private individual.'" To Constantine, Bk. 1, No. 2.

St. Basil ✠ 379.

St. Basil the Great, Metropolitan of Caesarea, a great theologian, an eloquent speaker, a masterly writer, but above all a man of indefatigable zeal for immortal souls, closed his most busy earthly career January 1, 379.

"Since the only begotten Son of God, our Lord and God Jesus Christ, by whom all things were made, declares, *I came down from heaven not to do my own will, but the will of him that sent me, even the Father's and of myself I do nothing*, and, *I have received a commandment what I should say, and what I should speak;* and as the Holy Ghost distributes gifts great and wonderful and worketh all in all, *speaketh nothing of himself, but whatsoever He shall hear from the Lord that He speaks;* how then, I ask, is it more necessary for the whole Church of God, careful *to keep the unity of the Spirit in the bond of peace*, to fulfill what is said in the Acts, *And the multitude of believers had but one heart and one soul;* for no one demanded that his own will be done, but all in common sought in the one Holy Spirit the will of that one Lord Jesus Christ, who says, *I come down from heaven, not to do my own will;* but the will of him that sent me, even the Father's, to whom he says, *not for them only do I pray but for them also who through the word believe in me, that they all may be one.*

"By these and many other testimonies which I pass over in silence, I am thus clearly and fully convinced that concord, agreeably to the will of Christ in the Holy Ghost, throughout the whole Church of God together, is necessary." On the Judgment of God, No. 4.

St. Ephraem ✝ 373.

St. Ephraem, the Syrian, is styled "doctor of the world," "lyre of the Holy Ghost," and "pillar of the Church." Many of his writings were read in the churches, as St. Jerome informs us. He is the author of numerous commentaries on Holy Scripture, and of the many poets of Christian Syria he is the most renowned; this "Prophet of the Syrians," as his admiring countrymen loved to call him, died in the year 373.

"Thou hast also built a Church on earth, which resembles the Church triumphant (in heaven); its foundations love impelled thee to lay, and grace presided at its completion. Thou hast also taken it as thy spouse, and hast made it thine at the price of thy blood. But since the wicked adversary of man, and his satellites and ministers, are striving to overthrow so glorious a structure, do thou, therefore, O Lord, guard it under thy protection, *that the gates of hell may not prevail against it;* that its inherent beauty perish not; that, in fine, its treasures, filled with every kind of wealth, fail not and be exhausted. Fulfill, O Lord, what thou didst promise to Peter, the prince of the apostles." Bk. 3, Paraeneses 62, Page 532.

The Catholic Church

"Blessed be the chosen one, who has chosen the Catholic Church, that holy lamb which the devouring wolf has not consumed. . . . Give heed, therefore, to my instructions, as my disciples, and depart not from the Catholic faith, which I also, having received it in my boyhood, have preserved immovable; neither turn aside from it in any doubt. And if any one separated, whoso goes, or turns aside, in opposition to God and his Holy Church, may he be forced down, breathing and living, into hell. . . . And if any one be lifted up against the Catholic Church, may he be smitten with leprosy, like the foolish Giezi." Book 2, Testament, No. 106-114.

St. Jerome ✠ 420.

St. Jerome, born at Stridon, 331, was baptized at Rome by Pope Liberius about 364 and ordained priest by bishop Paulinus of Antioch, 379. At the special request of Pope Damasus he undertook the monumental work of preparing a more accurate Latin text of the entire Bible. He died 420. He writes: "My resolution is to read the ancients, to try everything, to hold fast what is good and not to recede from the faith of the Catholic Church." Letter 119, to Minervius, No. 11.

"They shall not fall that dwell on the earth, and have their resting place in the Church, which is the abode of the Father, and the Son, and the Holy Ghost." Commentary on Isaias Book 8, 26; 18.

"*There stands one in the midst of you whom you know not;* and He will dwell there not for a short time, as in the synagogue, but for ever, as is verified in the Church of Christ." Comm. on Ezechiel 43; 9.

"As the lightning cometh out of the east, and appeareth even unto the west; so shall also the coming of the Son of man be. Go ye not out, believe not that the Son of man is either in the desert of the Gentiles, or in the *closets* of the heretics; but that *from the east even unto the west* His faith shineth in the Catholic churches." Comm. on Matt. 24; 27.

"The gates of hell shall not prevail against it. I consider the gates of hell to be the vices and sins, or at least the doctrines of heretics by which, being seduced, men are led to hell." Comm. on Matt. 16, 18, Bk. 3.

St. Augustine ✣ 430.

St. Augustine, Bishop of Hippo (died 430), by all odds the greatest of the ancient Fathers of the Church, and the greatest of its Doctors, possessed the creative power of a Tertullian, the ecclesiastical sentiments of a St. Cyprian, the dialectic precision of an Aristotle, the ideal speculative sublimity of a Plato, and a thorough knowledge of the human heart. He is the author of ninety-three works in two hundred and thirty-two books, without the many tracts and letters. Dr. O. Bardenhewer tells us: "He still passes for one of those mighty spirits that appear only at great intervals of time, but are destined to influence very powerfully the destiny of humanity. He has earned from all later generations the title of a Second Paul, a Doctor Gratiae. No Father of the Church has, even remotely so magisterially affected the entire later course of philosophy and theology, as Augustine did. With princely generosity he scattered along his way ideas in which later thinkers found the materials for entire systems of doctrine. . . . His writings are the faithful reflection of the teachings of the Church." Bardenhewer-Shahan, Patrology, page 495.

St. Augustine writes: "In the Catholic Church, not to mention that most sound wisdom, to the knowledge of which a few spiritual men attain in this life, so as to know it in a very small measure indeed, for they are but men, but still to know it without doubtfulness—for it is not quickness of understanding, but simplicity of belief, that makes the rest of the masses most safe,—not to mention, therefore, this wisdom, which you (Manichees) do not believe to be in the *Catholic Church*, many other things there are which most justly keep me in her fold. The agreement of peoples and of nations keep me; an authority begun with miracles, nourished with hope, increased with charity, strengthened by antiquity, keeps me; the succession of priests from the very chair of Peter the Apostle—unto whom the Lord after His resurrection committed His sheep to be fed—down even to the present pontificate keeps me; finally, the name itself of the *Catholic Church* keeps me,—a name which, in the midst of so many heresies, this Church alone has, not without cause, so held possession of as that, though all heretics would fain have themselves called Catholics, yet to the enquiry of any stranger:

Where is the assembly of the *Catholic Church* held? no heretic would dare to point out his own basilica or house. These ties of the Christian name, therefore, so numerous, so powerful, and most dear, justly keep a believing man in the *Catholic Church*." Against the Letter of Manichaeus, No. 5. "That Church assuredly is one, which our ancestors called the Catholic, that they might show by the name itself that it is throughout the whole world." On the Unity of the Church, No. 2. "The Christian religion is to be held by us, and the communion of that Church which is Catholic and is called Catholic not only by its own members, but also by all its adversaries. For in spite of themselves, even the very heretics, and disciples of schisms, when speaking not with their fellows, but with strangers, call the Catholic Church nothing else but the Catholic Church. For they cannot be understood, unless they distinguish her by that name by which she is called by the whole world." On the True Religion, No. 12.

St. Vincent of Lerin ✜ 450.

St. Vincent of Lerin, Priest and Monk (died about 450), was one of the more prominent theological writers of the fifth century. Under the pseudonym of Peregrinus he composed two highly esteemed Commonitoria. "While often inquiring with great earnestness and the utmost attention, of very many men excelling in holiness and learning, how I might, by some certain, and, as it were, general and undeviating way, discern the truth of *Catholic faith* from the falseness

The Catholic Church

of heretical pravity, I have received from almost all something like this answer: That whether I, or anyone else, would fain find out the deceptions, and avoid the snares of the heretics as they spring up, and remain safe and sound in the sound faith, he ought, in two ways, to fortify, with God's assistance, his faith. First, that is, *by the authority of the divine Law;* and then, by the tradition of the *Catholic Church.* Here some one perhaps may ask, 'Seeing that the Canon of the Scriptures is perfect, and of itself enough and more than enough for everything, what need is there that the authority of the Church's understanding be joined unto it?' The reason is, because all men do not take the Sacred Scripture, on account of its very profoundness, in one and the same sense; but this man and that man, in this way, and that way, interprets the sayings thereof; that as many opinions almost as there are men, would seem to be capable of being drawn therefrom. For Novatian expounds it in one way, in another Sabellius, in another Arius, Eunomius, Macedonius, in another Photinus, Apollinaris, Priscillian, in another Jovinian, Pelagius, Celestius, in another, in fine, Nestorius. And for this cause it is very necessary, on account of the many doublings of error so varied that the line of interpretation, both of prophets and apostles, be directed according to the rule of the ecclesiastical and Catholic sense. Again in the *Catholic Church* itself, very great care is to be taken that we hold that which hath been believed everywhere, always and by all men. For Catholic is truly and properly that, as the very force and meaning of the word declares, which comprises all things in general, after a universal manner; and this is thus, in fine, attained,—if we follow *universality, antiquity, consent*. Now, we follow *universality* thus,—if we confess this one faith to be true, which the whole Church throughout the world confesses,—*antiquity*, thus, if we in no wise recede from the senses which it is manifest that our holy elders and Fathers openly manifested,—*consent*, likewise in the same manner, if, in this antiquity itself, we adhere to the definitions and sentiments of all, or at least of nearly all the priests and doctors together.

What then shall a Catholic Christian do, if some small part of the Church cut itself off from the communion of the universal faith? What, indeed, but prefer the healthiness of the whole body before the pestiferous and corrupt member? What if some novel contagion attempt to taint no longer a small part only, but the whole Church alike? Then, likewise, shall he see to it that he cleave unto antiquity, which is now utterly incapable of being seduced by any craft of novelty. What, if in antiquity itself, there be discovered some error of two or three men, or of some one city or province even? Then he shall by all means give heed that he prefer, before the temerity or ignorance of a few, the decrees, if such there be of a general council, universally received of old. What, if some such case arise, wherein nothing of this nature can be found? Then shall he bestow his labor to consult and interrogate the collated sentiments of the ancients,—

The Catholic Church

of those, to wit, who, though living at different times and places, yet remaining in the union and faith of the one Catholic Church, were trust-worthy teachers; and whatsoever he shall recognize that not one or two only, but all alike, with one unvarying consent, plainly, frequently, unswervingly held, wrote, taught, that, let him understand, is to be believed by him without any doubt. . . .

To announce, therefore, to Catholic Christians, anything besides that which they have received, never was lawful, never will be lawful; and to anathematize those who announce anything besides that which has been once received, was never otherwise than needful, is everywhere needful, ever will be needful. Which being so, is there any one of so great audacity as to teach besides that which has been taught in the Church; or of such levity as to receive anything besides that which he has received from the Church? There cries aloud, and he cries aloud again and again, to all men, to all times, and to all places he cries aloud by his epistles, that vessel of election (St. Paul), that master of the Gentiles . . . that if any one announce a new dogma, let him be anathematized . . . Oftentimes pondering and reflecting on these self-same things, I cannot sufficiently marvel that such is the madness of some men, such the impiety of their blinded understanding, such, in fine, their lust after error, that they be not content with the rule of belief once delivered and received from antiquity, but do daily seek after something new, and ever be longing to add something to religion, to change, to take away; as though it were not a doctrine from heaven, which once revealed suffices, but an earthly institution, which cannot otherwise be perfected than by continuous amendment, yea, rather, correction; whereas the divine oracles cry out, *Do not transfer the bounds which thy fathers have set;* and, *Do not judge over the judge;* and, *The serpent shall bite him that breaketh the hedge;* and that apostolic saying by which all wicked novelties of all heresies have often, as a kind of spiritual sword, been cut off, and ever will be cut off: *O Timothy, keep that which is committed to thy trust, avoiding the profane novelties of words, and oppositions of knowledge falsely so called, which some promising, have erred concerning the faith . . . Avoid,* he says, *the profane novelties of words;* he did not say, avoid antiquities; he did not say, avoid ancientness; yea, rather, he shows what contrariwise he should follow. For if *novelty* is to be *avoided,* antiquity is to be held to; and if *novelty* be *profane,* antiquity is sacred . . . But it is worth while to handle with great care the whole passage of the Apostle: *O Timothy, keep that which is committed to thy trust avoiding the profane novelties of words!* Who is at this day Timothy? But either generally, the universal Church, or specially, the whole body of prelates, who ought either themselves to have a complete knowledge of divine worship, or who ought to infuse it into others. What is, *Keep the deposit?* Keep it, he says, for fear of thieves, for fear of enemies, lest, while men sleep, they oversow cockle upon that good seed

The Catholic Church

of wheat, which the Son of man had sowed in His field. *Keep,* he says, *the depositum.* What is the depositum? that is that which is committed to thee, not that which is invented by thee; what thou hast received, not what thou hast devised; a thing not of wit, but of doctrine, not of private assumption, but of public tradition; a thing brought to thee, not brought forth by thee; wherein thou must not be an author, but a keeper; not a beginner, but a disciple; not a leader, but a follower. The depositum, he says, keep; preserve the talent of Catholic faith inviolate and untouched; that which is entrusted to thee, let that remain with thee, let that be delivered by thee. . . . But, haply, some one says, shall we then have no advancement of religion in the Church of Christ? Let us have it indeed, and the greatest. For who is he, so envious of men so hateful to God, as to hinder this? But yet in such sort that it be truly an advancement of faith, not a change. Seeing that it is the nature of an advancement, that in itself each thing grow greater; but of a change that something be turned from one thing into another. Wherefore the understanding, knowledge, wisdom, as well of each as of all, as well of one man as of the whole Church, ought, with the advance of times and ages, to increase and go forward abundantly and earnestly; but in its own kind only, in the same doctrine, to wit, in the same sense, and in the same sentiment. Let the soul's religion imitate the law of the body which as years go on, develops indeed, and opens out its due proportions and yet remains identically what it was.

So also the doctrine of the Christian religion must follow those laws of advancement; namely, that with years it be consolidated, with time it be expanded, with age it be exalted; yet remain uncorrupt and untouched and be full and perfect in all the proportions of each of its parts, and with all its members, as it were, and proper senses; that it admit no change besides, sustain no loss of its propriety, no variety of its definition." 1 Commonitorium, No. 1-29 passim.

Questions on the Text

1. Who was St. Clement?
2. Whom did he succeed as Pope?
3. What does he say about the activity of the Apostles?
4. Whose disciple was St. Ignatius?
5. What does he emphasize in his letter to the Ephesians?
6. Which were the last words of St. Polycarp to his judge?
7. Who was St. Justin?
8. What does St. Irenaeus write about the extension of the Church?
9. Give his enumeration of the Popes.
10. What does Origen say about St. Peter?
11. Tertullian says: "That is truest which is most ancient." To what does he apply this reasoning?
12. What does Lactantius say about the Catholic Church?
13. For what is Eusebius specially known?
14. What does St. Athanasius say concerning tradition?
15. To what does St. Hilary attribute the appointment of St. Peter as head of the Church?
16. Who is St. Basil?
17. What has St. Cyprian to say about those who choose the Catholic Church?
18. What did St. Jerome understand by "the gates of hell?"
19. What does St. Augustine say anent the Catholic Church?
20. Give the main argument of St. Vincent Lerin for discerning the true Church.

List of Roman Pontiffs

⇉⋙ ⋘⇇

1. ST. PETER, of Bethsaida in Galilee, Prince of the Apostles, who received from Jesus Christ the Supreme Pontifical Power to be transmitted to his Successors; resided first at Antioch, then at Rome, where he was martyred in the year 67.

	Appointed	Died
1. St. Peter	33	67

	Elected	Died
2. St. Linus, M.	67	78
3. St. Cletus, M.	78	90
4. St. Clement I., M.	90	100
5. St. Anacletus, M.	100	112
6. St. Evaristus, M.	112	121
7. St. Alexander I., M.	121	132
8. St. Sixtus I., M.	132	142
9. St. Telesphorus, M.	142	154
10. St. Hyginus, M.	154	158
11. St. Pius I., M.	158	167
12. St. Anicetus, M.	167	175
13. St. Soterus, M.	175	182
14. St. Eleutherius, M.	182	193
15. St. Victor I., M.	193	203
16. St. Zephyrinus, M.	203	221
17. St. Callistus I., M.	221	227
18. St. Urban I., M.	227	233
19. St. Pontian, M.	233	238
20. St. Anterus, M.	238	239
21. St. Fabian, M.	239	253
22. St. Cornelius, M.	253	255
23. St. Lucius I., M.	255	257
24. St. Stephen I., M.	257	260
25. St. Sixtus II., M.	260	261
26. St. Dionysius	261	272
27. St. Felix I., M.	272	275
28. St. Eutychian, M.	275	283
29. St. Caius, M.	283	296
30. St. Marcellinus, M.	296	304
31. St. Marcellus I., M.	304	309
32. St. Eusebius	309	311
33. St. Melchiades	311	313
34. St. Sylvester I.	314	337
35. St. Mark	337	340
36. St. Julius I.	341	352
37. St. Liberius	352	366
38. St. Felix II.*	363	365
39. St. Damasus I.	367	384
40. St. Siricius	384	398
41. St. Anastasius I.	399	402
42. St. Innocent I.	402	417
43. St. Zozimus	417	418
44. St. Boniface I.	418	423
45. St. Celestine I.	423	432
46. St. Sixtus III.	432	440
47. St. Leo I. (the Great)	440	461
48. St. Hilary	461	468
49. St. Simplicius	468	483
50. St. Felix III.	483	492
51. St. Gelasius I.	492	496
52. St. Anastasius II.	496	498
53. St. Symmachus	498	514
54. St. Hormisdas	514	523
55. St. John I.	523	526
56. St. Felix IV.	526	530
57. Boniface II.	530	532
58. John II.	532	535
59. St. Agapitus	535	536
60. St. Silverius, M.	536	538
61. Vigilius	538	555
62. Pelagius I.	555	560
63. John III.	560	573
64. Benedict I.	574	578
65. Pelagius II.	578	590
66. St. Gregory I. (the Great)	590	604
67. Sabinian	604	606

*—Pope during exile of Liberius.

	Elected	Died
68. Boniface III	607	607
69. St. Boniface IV	608	615
70. St. Deusdedit I	615	619
71. Boniface V	619	625
72. Honorius I	625	638
73. Serverinus	639	640
74. John IV	640	642
75. Theodore I	642	649
76. St. Martin I., M	649	655
77. St. Eugene I	655	657
78. St. Vatalian	657	672
79. Adeodatus II	672	676
80. Donus I	676	678
81. St. Agatho	678	682
82. St. Leo II	682	683
83. St. Benedict II	684	685
84. John V	685	686
85. Conon	686	687
86. St. Sergius I	687	701
87. John VI	701	705
88. John VII	705	707
89. Sisinnius	708	708
90. Constantine	708	715
91. St. Gregory II	715	731
92. St. Gregory III	731	741
93. St. Zachary	741	752
94. Stephen II.†	752	752
95. St. Stephen III	752	757
96. St. Paul I	757	767
97. Stephen IV	768	771
98. Adrian I	771	795
99. St. Leo III	795	816
100. St. Stephen V	816	817
101. St. Paschal I	817	824
102. Eugene II	824	827
103. Valentine	827	827
104. Gregory IV	827	844
105. Sergius II	844	847
106. St. Leo IV	847	855
107. Benedict III	855	858
108. St. Nicolas I. (the Great)	858	867
109. Adrian II	867	872
110. John VIII	872	882
111. Marinus I	882	884
112. St. Adrian III	884	885
113. Stephen VI	885	891
114. Formosus	891	896
115. Stephen VII	896	897
116. Romanus	897	898
117. Theodore II	898	898

†—Died before his consecration.

	Elected	Died
118. John IX	898	900
119. Benedict IV	900	903
120. Leo V	903	903
121. Christopher	903	904
122. Sergius III	904	911
123. Anastasius III	911	913
124. Landus	913	914
125. John X	915	928
126. Leo VI	928	929
127. Stephen VIII	929	931
128. John XI	931	936
129. Leo VII	936	939
130. Stephen IX	939	942
131. Marinus II	942	946
132. Agapitus II	946	956
133. John XII	956	964
134. Benedict V	964	965
135. John XIII	965	972
136. Benedict VI	972	973
137. Donus II	973	973
138. Benedict VII	975	984
139. John XIV	984	985
140. John XV	985	996
141. Gregory V	996	999
142. Sylvester II	999	1003
143. John XVI or XVII	1003	1003
144. John XVII or XVIII	1003	1009
145. Sergius IV	1009	1012
146. Benedict VIII	1012	1024
147. John XVIII or XIX or XX	1024	1033
148. Benedict IX	1033	1044
149. Gregory VI	1044	1046
150. Clement II	1046	1047
151. Damasus II	1048	1048
152. St. Leo IX	1049	1054
153. Victor II	1055	1057
154. Stephen X	1057	1058
155. Nicholas II	1059	1061
156. Alexander II	1061	1073
157. St. Gregory VII	1073	1085
158. B. Victor III	1087	1087
159. B. Urban II	1088	1099
160. Paschal II	1099	1118
161. Gelasius II	1118	1119
162. Callistus II	1119	1124
163. Honorius II	1124	1130
164. Innocent II	1130	114
165. Celestine II	1143	114
166. Lucius II	1144	114
167. B. Eugene III	1145	115

	Elected	Died
168. Anastasius IV	1153	1154
169. Adrian IV	1154	1159
170. Alexander III	1159	1181
171. Lucius III	1181	1185
172. Urban III	1185	1187
173. Gregory VIII	1187	1187
174. Clement III	1187	1191
175. Celestine III	1191	1198
176. Innocent III	1198	1216
177. Honorius III	1216	1227
178. Gregory IX	1227	1241
179. Celestine IV	1241	1241
180. Innocent IV	1243	1254
181. Alexander IV	1254	1261
182. Urban IV	1261	1264
183. Clement IV	1265	1268
184. B. Gregory X	1271	1276
185. B. Innocent V	1276	1276
186. Adrian V	1276	1276
187. John XIX or XX or XXI	1276	1277
188. Nicholas III	1277	1280
189. Martin IV	1281	1285
190. Honorius IV	1285	1287
191. Nicholas IV	1288	1292
192. St. Celestine V	1294	‡1294
193. Boniface VIII	1294	1303
194. B. Benedict X or XI	1303	1304
195. Clement V	1305	1314
196. John XX or XXI or XXII	1316	1334
197. Benedict XI or XII	1334	1342
198. Clement VI	1342	1352
199. Innocent VI	1352	1362
200. B. Urban V	1362	1370
201. Gregory XI	1370	1378
202. Urban VI	1378	1389
203. Boniface IX	1389	1404
204. Innocent VII	1404	1406
205. Gregory XII	1406	‡1409
206. Alexander V	1409	1410
207. John XXII or XXIII or XXIV	1410	‡1415
208. Martin III or V	1417	1431
209. Eugene IV	1431	1447
210. Nicholas V	1447	1455
211. Callistus III	1455	1458
212. Pius II	1458	1464
213. Paul II	1464	1471

‡—Resigned.

	Elected	Died
214. Sixtus IV	1471	1484
215. Innocent VIII	1484	1492
216. Alexander VI	1492	1503
217. Pius III	1503	1503
218. Julius II	1503	1513
219. Leo X	1513	1521
220. Adrian VI	1522	1523
221. Clement VII	1523	1534
222. Paul III	1534	1549
223. Julius III	1550	1555
224. Marcellus II	1555	1555
225. Paul IV	1555	1559
226. Pius IV	1559	1565
227. St. Pius V	1566	1572
228. Gregory XIII	1572	1585
229. Sixtus V	1585	1590
230. Urban VII	1590	1590
231. Gregory XIV	1590	1591
232. Innocent IX	1591	1591
233. Clement VIII	1592	1605
234. Leo XI	1605	1605
235. Paul V	1605	1621
236. Gregory XV	1621	1623
237. Urban VIII	1623	1644
238. Innocent X	1644	1655
239. Alexander VII	1655	1667
240. Clement IX	1667	1669
241. Clement X	1670	1676
242. Innocent XI	1676	1689
243. Alexander VIII	1689	1691
244. Innocent XII	1691	1700
245. Clement XI	1700	1721
246. Innocent XIII	1721	1724
247. Benedict XIII	1724	1730
248. Clement XII	1730	1740
249. Benedict XIV	1740	1758
250. Clement XIII	1758	1769
251. Clement XIV	1769	1774
252. Pius VI	1775	1799
253. Pius VII	1800	1823
254. Leo XII	1823	1829
255. Pius VIII	1829	1830
256. Gregory XVI	1831	1846
257. Pius IX	1846	1878
258. Leo XIII	1878	1903
259. Pius X	1903	1914
260. Benedict XV	1914	1922
261. Pius XI	1922	

CHRONOLOGICAL LIST OF POPES AS PROOF OF THE APOSTOLICITY AND CONTINUITY OF THE CATHOLIC CHURCH.

The continuity of any government may be ascertained by the uninterrupted succession of its chief executives. Upon the Declaration of Independence, July 4th, 1776, followed the gradual development of a new republic, of which George Washington was elected the first president in 1789. Now if I should want to prove to any one seeking such information, that the same republic is still in existence, the simplest way of doing this would be to establish the legitimate claim of the present chief executive of this glorious republic to his rights as chief magistrate. This I can do by showing that he was legally elected to the presidency, which office, though successively held by many, has never been abolished, nor has it ever been vacant for any considerable time. In other words, by enumerating the names of all its presidents, I prove the continuity of the republic of which they were presidents.

Similarly, the enumeration of the chief executives of the Catholic Church, the bishops of Rome, engenders the conviction of the uninterrupted existence of the Catholic Church from the days of Jesus Christ until the present moment. As we saw in the preceding articles Jesus Christ appointed St. Peter as head of His Church. From Antioch, where the Prince of the Apostles was the first bishop, he came to Rome and established his see in the Eternal City. As head of the Church, St. Peter is called Pope. All his legitimate successors in the episcopal see of Rome hold the same supreme jurisdiction over the entire Catholic Church.

Should any one of my readers feel inclined to doubt the correctness of the names or the chronology of the list, I ask him in all kindness to consult any reliable historian or any standard encyclopedia and compare results.

Since quite a number of the Popes went by the same name, it will not be considered superfluous to remark that it was only since the 13th century that the Popes began to add numbers to their names; Urban IV., 1261-1264, began this. Hence the enumeration of Popes with the same name of earlier date is the work of historians.

The Seven Sacraments

SACRAMENTS are visible signs permanently instituted by our Lord Jesus Christ, which signs signify and confer grace. They are channels of grace and thus become means of sanctity. Jesus Christ instituted the following seven sacraments: Baptism, Confirmation, the Holy Eucharist, Penance, Extreme Unction, Holy Orders, and Matrimony. Ever since the time of Christ these seven sacraments have been and still are in the Catholic Church.

I. BAPTISM.

The sacrament of Baptism—or, if it cannot be actually received, a desire for the same—is indispensably necessary for salvation. Jesus himself has said: *"Amen, amen I say to thee, unless a man be born again of water and the Holy Ghost, he cannot enter into the kingdom of God."* St. John 3:5. Shortly before His glorious ascension into heaven, He commissioned His Apostles: "Going therefore, teach ye all nations; *baptizing them in the name of the Father, and of the Son, and of the Holy Ghost."* St. Matt. 28:19.

On the day on which the Holy Ghost came down upon the Apostles devout men, out of every nation under heaven, amazed and wondering over the things which they saw and heard, "said to Peter, and to the rest of the Apostles: What shall we do, men and brethren? But Peter said to them: Do penance, and *be baptized every one of you* in the name of Jesus Christ, for the remission of your sins." Acts 2:37, 38. When Saul heard the voice of Jesus Christ: "Saul, Saul, why persecutest thou me?" Saul converted. "And (Ananias) laying his hands upon him, he said: Brother Saul, the Lord Jesus hath sent me, he that appeared to thee in the way as thou camest; that thou mayest receive thy sight, and be filled with the Holy Ghost. And immediately there fell from his eyes as it were scales, and he received his sight; and rising up, *he was baptized.*" Acts 9:17, 18. "Then Peter answered: *Can any man forbid water that these should not be baptized,* who had received the Holy Ghost as well as we? And he commanded them to be baptized in the name of the Lord Jesus Christ." Acts 10:47, 48.

In the famous *Didache,* or *Teaching of the Twelve Apostles,* which dates back to the first century, we find the following extract on baptism: "Now concerning baptism, thus shall you baptize: Baptize in the name of the Father and of the Son and of the Holy Ghost in flowing water. But if you have no flowing water, then baptize in other water. And if it be impossible to do so in cold water, then use warm water. But if you have neither (i. e., a sufficient quantity for baptism by immersion), then *pour water on the head* thrice in the name of the Father and of the Son and of the Holy Ghost." Chap. VII.

St. Justin (died about 167) speaking of the

catechumens, writes: "They are then conducted by us to a place where there is water and are regenerated in the same manner of regeneration in which we ourselves have been regenerated. For in the name of God the Father and Lord of the universe, and of our Savior Jesus Christ, and of the Holy Spirit, they then receive baptism in the water. For Christ has said: *Unless you shall have been born again you shall not enter the kingdom of heaven.*" 1 Apology, No. 61.

St. Irenaeus (died about 202): "And giving to the disciples the power of regeneration unto God, he said to them: *Going, teach all nations, baptizing them in the name of the Father and of the Son and of the Holy Ghost.*" Against Heresies, Bk. 3, Chap. 17. "For He came to save all men through himself: all, I repeat, who through Him, are born again unto God; infants, children, youths, men, and old age. Therefore did He pass through every age; an infant with the infants to sanctify infants; with the children a child to sanctify those of that age." Against Heresies, Bk. 2, Chap. 22, No. 4.

Origen (died about 254): "*The Church has received from the Apostles the tradition to confer baptism upon little children.*" Commentary on Ep. to the Romans, Bk. V, No. 9.

St. Cyprian (died 258): "Now as to the case of infants, who, you say, ought not to be baptized within the second or third day after birth, and that the law of the ancient circumcision ought to be had regard to, so that, in your opinion, the new-born child ought not to be baptized and hallowed before the eighth day; it

The Catholic Church

has seemed far otherwise to our council. For not one agreed to what you thought ought to be done; but we all, on the contrary, judged that to no man born the mercy and grace of God ought to be denied." Letter 59 to Fidus, No. 2.

St. Athanasius (373): "For what is said in the Epistle to the Hebrews (6:4) does not exclude sinners from repentance, but shows that *the baptism of the Catholic Church is one*, and not twofold." Letter IV. to Serapion, No. 13.

St. Cyril of Jerusalem (386): "Verily, great is the baptism which is before you; it is a ransom for the captives; the remission of guilt; the death of sin; the soul's regeneration; a garment of light; a holy seal indissoluble; a chariot to heaven; the joy of paradise; the cause of obtaining the kingdom; the gift of adoption." Procatechesis, No. 16.

St. Pacian (died 390): "The sin of Adam had passed unto the whole race: *For by one man*, says the apostle, *sin entered, and by sin death, and so (death) passed upon all men*. Therefore, the justice of Christ also must needs pass unto the human race. . . . Christ begets in the Church by means of His priests, as says the same Apostle, *In Christ have I begotten you*. . . . These things cannot be otherwise fulfilled than by the sacrament of the laver and of the chrism and of the bishop. For by the laver, sins are cleansed away; by chrism, the Holy Spirit is poured upon us; but both these we obtain at the hand and mouth of the bishop; and thus the whole man is born again and is renewed in Christ." Sermon on Baptism, No. 5, 6.

St. Jerome (died 420): Pelagian: "Tell me, pray, why infants are baptized?" Catholic: "That the sins may be forgiven them in baptism." Dialogue against the Pelagians, Bk. 3, No. 18.

St. Augustine (died 430): "As none is prohibited from receiving baptism, from the child just born even to the decrepit old man, so there is none that does not die to sin in baptism; infants, however, to original sin only, but adults die also to all those sins, which by living ill they have added to that which they derived from their birth." Enchiridion, No. 43.

II. Confirmation.

In Baptism we are made the temples of the Holy Ghost, but in Confirmation we receive the Holy Ghost in all the plenitude of His graces. This sacrament conferred on baptized persons strengthens them in the profession of the Christian faith. Though our Lord had given the Holy Ghost to His Apostles, nevertheless they remained fearful until Pentecost-day, when the Holy Ghost with the plenitude of His graces came upon them. Then they were confirmed, strengthened in their faith and feared not to face the enemies of Christ and to preach the gospel of salvation.

"Now when the Apostles, who were in Jerusalem, had heard that Samaria had received the word of God, they sent unto them Peter and John. Who, when they were come, prayed for them, that they might receive the Holy Ghost. For He was not as yet come upon any of them; but they were only baptized in the name of the Lord Jesus. *Then they laid their hands upon them, and they received the Holy Ghost.*" Acts 8:14:17. In Ephesus St. Paul had administered confirmation. "And when Paul had imposed his hands on them, the Holy Ghost came upon them." Acts 19:6.

St. Jerome (died 420): "I do not deny that it is the custom of the churches, for the bishop to journey to those who have been baptized by priests and deacons, at a distance from the greater cities, to impose hands upon them to invoke the Holy Ghost." Dialogue against the Luciferians, No. 9.

St. Isidore of Pelusium (died about 440): "Philip did indeed baptize those who had become disciples at Samaria, but the Apostles Peter and John, having come unto them from Jerusalem, delivered unto them the grace of the Holy Spirit. Whereas he but baptized as a disciple, whilst the Apostles, upon whom the authority to give it had been conferred, complete the grace." Bk. 1, Letter 350, P. 114.

St. Innocent I., Pope (died 417): "That this high-priestly office, namely, that they may seal, or deliver the Spirit, the Paraclete, belongs to the bishops, is demonstrated not only by ecclesiastical usage, but also by that passage of the Acts of the Apostles, wherein it is declared that Peter and John were sent to confer the Holy Ghost upon those that had already been baptized." Letter 25th, Chap. 3, No. 6.

III. THE HOLY EUCHARIST.

The Holy Eucharist is the true Body and Blood of Jesus Christ under the appearance of bread and wine for the nourishment of our souls.

The day after the multiplication of loaves, Jesus spoke to the multitude in the synagogue at Capharnaum: "The bread that I will give, is my flesh, for the life of the world. The Jews therefore strove among themselves, saying: How can this man give us his flesh to eat? Then Jesus said to them: Amen, amen I say unto you: Except you eat the flesh of the Son of man, and drink his blood, you shall not have life in you. He that eateth my flesh, and drinketh my blood, hath everlasting life; and I will raise him up in the last day. For my flesh is meat indeed: and my blood is drink indeed. He that eateth my flesh, and drinketh my blood, abideth in me, and I in him. As the living Father hath sent me, and I live by the Father; so he that eateth me, the same also shall live by me." John 6:52-58.

"And whilst they were at supper, Jesus took bread, and blessed, and broke; and gave to his disciples, and said: Take ye, and eat. This is my body. And taking the chalice, he gave thanks, and gave to them, saying: Drink ye all of this. For this is my blood of the new testament, which shall be shed for many unto remission of sins." St. Matt. 26:26-28. "And taking bread, he gave thanks and brake; and gave to them, saying: This is my body, which is given for you. Do this for a commemoration of me. In like manner the chalice also, after he had supped, saying: This is the chalice, the new testament in my blood, which shall be shed for you." St. Luke 22:19, 20.

The Apostles did what they were commanded to

do: change bread and wine into the body and blood of Jesus Christ in commemoration of Him. St. Paul asks the following question: "The chalice of benediction, which we bless, is it not the communion of the blood of Christ? And the bread, which we break, is it not the partaking of the body of the Lord?" 1 Cor. 10:16.

St. Ignatius (died about 107): "I desire God's bread, heavenly bread, the bread of life, which is the flesh of Jesus Christ, the Son of God, who has been of the seed of David and Abraham: and as drink I desire His blood, which is love incorruptible and life everlasting." Letter to the Romans, No. 7. "Strive, therefore, to partake of one Eucharist; for one is the flesh of our Lord Jesus Christ, and one is the chalice, unto the union with His blood." Philadelphians, 4.

Tertullian (died about 240): "The body feeds upon the flesh and blood of Christ, that the soul also may be nurtured of God." On the Resurrection of the Body, Chap. 8.

St. Cyprian, Bishop of Carthage (died 258): "A harder and fiercer battle is at hand, for which Christ's soldiers must prepare themselves by faith untainted and resolute courage; bearing in mind that therefore do they daily drink the chalice of the blood of Christ, that they themselves, too, may be able to pour forth their blood for Christ." Letter 56th to the Thibaritans, No. 1.

St. Hilary (died 366): "For what we say concerning the natural verity (very nature) of Christ in us, we say foolishly and impiously unless we have learned it from Him. For He himself says, *My flesh is truly meat, and my blood is truly drink. He that eateth my flesh and drinketh my blood abideth in me, and I in him.* There is no room left for doubting the verity of the flesh and blood. For now it is truly flesh, and it is truly blood; both according to the declaration of the Lord himself, and according to our faith; and these being received and drunk, effect this, that both we are in Christ, and Christ is in us." On the Trinity, Bk. 8, Chap. 14.

St. Cyril of Jerusalem (d. 386): "In the figure of bread is given to thee the Body and in the figure of wine the Blood, so that when thou receivest the Body and Blood of Christ, thou mayest become of one body and one blood with Him; for thus we shall become Christbearers, when His Body and His Blood are distributed in our members." Catechesis, 22:3. "What appears to be bread is not bread, although it seems thus to taste, but it is the Body of Christ, and what appears to be wine, is not wine, although the taste judgeth thus, but it is the Blood of Christ." Catechesis, 22:9.

St. Basil (d. 379): "With what fear, with what conviction, with what disposition, should we partake of the Body and Blood of Christ? The fear is taught us by the Apostle, when he says: *He that eateth and drinketh unworthily, eateth and drinketh judgment to himself.* The faith in the words of the Lord produce *full conviction,* seeing that He says, *This is my Body which is given for you. Do this for a commemoration of me;* as also the faith in the testimony of John, who, having first declared the glory of the Word, then introduced the manner of His incarnation, saying, that *The Word was made flesh and dwelt amongst us, and we saw His glory*, etc.; and the faith also in the words of the Apostle, writing: *Who being in the form of God*, etc. When, therefore, the soul putting faith in these and similar important words, has learned the greatness of His humility and obedience, that one so great obeyed the Father even unto death, for the sake of our life; I am of opinion that the soul's affections will be aroused to love both God the Father, *who spared not His own Son, but delivered Him up for us all*, and also His only begotten Son, *who became obedient even unto death* for our redemption and salvation; such a disposition and preparation ought he to have who partakes of the Bread and the Cup." From his Rules, Briefly Discussed. Question 172.

St. Ambrose, Bishop of Milan (d. 397): "Perhaps thou wilt say, 'I see a different thing: how is it that you assert that I shall receive the Body of Christ?' It yet remains to prove this also. How many examples shall we use? Let us prove that this is not what nature formed, but what the benediction has consecrated; and that the force of the benediction is greater than the force of nature, because, by the blessing, even nature itself is changed." On the Mysteries, Chap. 9.

St. Chrysostom, Patriarch of Constantinople (d. 407): "Reflect, O man, what a sacrifice thou art about to touch; what a table thou art about to approach; consider, that—though dust and ashes—thou receivest Christ's Body and Blood. What the Lord did not tolerate on the cross, He tolerates now in the sacrifice through love of thee; He permits himself to be broken in pieces that all may be filled to satiety." Homily 24th on 1 Cor., No. 2.

"Believe that there takes place now the same banquet as that in which Christ sat at table and that this banquet is in no way different from that. For it is not true that this banquet is prepared by a man, while that was prepared by Himself, but both this banquet and that one are prepared by Himself." Homily 50 on Matt., No. 3.

"Today, as then, it is the Lord, who worketh and offereth all." Hom. 27th on 1 Cor., No. 4. "We assume the role of servants; it is He who consecrates and transmutes." Hom. 82 on Matt., No. 5. "It is not man who causes what is present to become the Body and Blood of Christ, but Christ Himself who was crucified for us. The priest is the representative when he pronounces those words; but the power and the grace are those of the Lord. He says: *This is my Body*. This word changes the things that lie before us." Homily 1 on the Betrayal of Judas, No. 6.

St. Nilus (died about 430): "Indeed, before the prayer of the priest and the descent of the Holy Ghost, the things that lie to open view are plain bread and common wine; but after these awful invocations and the advent of the adorable and vivifying and good Spirit, the things that lie upon the holy table are no longer plain bread and common wine, but the precious and immaculate Body and Blood of Christ, the God of all, which (Body and Blood) purify from every defilement those who partake thereof with much fear and eagerness." Letters, 1 Book.

Theodoret, Bishop of Cyrus (d. 458): "For no man ever hateth his own flesh, but nourisheth and cherisheth it, as Christ does the Church, nourishing and cherishing it, and giving it His own Body and Blood. Because we are members of His Body. For as Eve was formed out of Adam, so are we out of Christ the Lord: for we are buried with Him in baptism, and we rise together with Him; and *we eat His Body, and we drink His Blood.*" Commentary on Epistle to Ephesians.

IV. Penance.

Through the Sacrament of Penance the sins committed after baptism are forgiven. The repentant Christian confesses his sins sincerely to a duly authorized priest, who hears the sins, gives an admonition and, if he considers the penitent rightly disposed (i. e., contrite and determined to avoid the sin in future and to make satisfaction for the sins of injustice), gives absolution. The priest absolves in the place of God, whose representative he is. The power to absolve from sins and the right to refuse absolution, Jesus Christ gave to His Apostles and to their rightful successors. Duly authorized Priests have this double power.

"Now when it was late that same day, the first of the week, and the doors were shut, where the disciples were gathered together, for fear of the Jews, Jesus came and stood in the midst, and said to them: Peace be to you. And when he had said this, he shewed them his hands and his side. The disciples therefore were glad, when they saw the Lord. He said therefore to them again: Peace be to you. As the Father hath sent me, I also send you. When he had said this, he breathed on them; and he said to them: *Receive ye the Holy Ghost. Whose sins you shall forgive, they are forgiven them; and whose sins you shall retain, they are retained.*" St. John 20:19-23. The power of the Apostles to forgive and to retain sins is still within the Church.

St. Ephraem (died 373): "The exalted dignity of the priesthood is far above our understanding and the power of speech. Consider that remission of sins is not given to mortals without the venerable priesthood." Sermon on the Priesthood, No. 3.

St. Ambrose (died 397): "God makes no distinction; he promised His mercy to all; and granted to His priests permission to loose without exception." On Penitence, Bk. 1, Chap. 3. "If it be not lawful that sins be forgiven by man, why do you baptize? For assuredly in baptism there is remission of all sins." On Penit., Bk. 1, Chap. 8. "It seems impossible that water should wash away sin; furthermore, Naaman, the Syrian, believed not that his leprosy could be cured by water. But God, who has given us so great a grace, rendered possible the impossible. In the same manner it seemed impossible that sins should be forgiven by penitence; Christ granted this to His

Apostles, which from the Apostles has been transmitted to the offices of the priests." On Penitence, Bk. 2, Chap. 2.

St. Chrysostom (died 407): "Men that dwell on earth, and have their abode therein, have had committed to them the dispensation of the things that are in heaven, and have received the power which God has not given either to angels or to archangels; for not to these was it said, *Whatsoever you shall bind on earth, shall be bound also in heaven; and whatsoever you shall loose upon earth, shall be loosed also in heaven.* They that rule on earth have indeed power to *bind,* but the body only; whereas *this* bond touches the very soul itself, and reaches even unto heaven; and whatsoever the priests do here below, the same does God ratify above, and the Lord confirms the sentence of His servants. And what else is this, but that He has given them all heavenly power? For, saith He: *Whose sins you shall forgive, they are forgiven, and whose sins you shall retain, they are retained.*" On the Priesthood, Book 3d, No. 5.

St. Peter Chrysologus (died about 450): "*Whose sins you shall forgive,* etc. He gave the power of forgiving sins; He by His own breath infused into their hearts, and bestowed on them the very forgiver of sins Himself. *When He said this, he breathed on them, saying, Receive ye the Holy Ghost,* etc. Where are those who deny that sins can be forgiven by men? Who completely crush the fallen, that they may not arise; who, with a cruel spirit, withdraw the remedy from the sickness and withhold the medicine from the wounds? Who impiously insult sinners with the despair of a return? Peter forgives sins, and receives the penitent with all joy, and avails himself of this power which God has granted to all priests." Sermon 84.

V. EXTREME UNCTION.

With holy oil consecrated by the bishop, the priest anoints the sick Christian in the form of a cross on the five senses: eyes, ears, nose, mouth, hands and feet. In case of urgent need, the dying Christian is anointed under one form; the priest anoints the forehead of the dying.

St. James, one of the twelve Apostles, writes: "Is any man sick among you? Let him bring in the priests of the Church, and let them pray over him, anointing him with oil in the name of the Lord. And the prayer of faith shall save the sick man: and the Lord shall raise him up: and if he be in sins, they shall be forgiven him." St. James 5:14, 15.

St. Caesarius, Archbishop of Arles (died 543), to whom the best critics attribute many of the Pseudo-Augustinian Sermons, writes: "As often as any infirmity supervenes, let him who is sick receive the Body and Blood of Christ; and then anoint his body, that that which is written may be accomplished in him; *Is any one sick? Let him bring in the priests, and let them pray over him, anointing him with oil,* etc. See, brethren, that he, who in sickness has recourse to the Church, shall deserve to obtain both health of body and pardon of sins." Sermon 265, No. 3 (in Appendice St. Augustini).

St. Innocent (died 417): "You have set down what is written in the Epistle of the blessed Apostle James, *Is any one sick among you? Let him call the priests, and let them pray over him, anointing him with oil in the name of the Lord, and the prayer of faith shall save the sick man, and the Lord shall raise him up, and if he has committed sin, he shall pardon him.* This, without doubt, ought to be understood, of the faithful who are sick, who can be anointed with the holy oil of chrism, which, having been prepared by the bishop, may be used not only for priests, but for all Christians, for anointing in their own need or in that of their relations." Letter 25th, Chap. 8, No. 11.

VI. Holy Orders.

The priesthood is preceded by four minor and two major Orders. The Minor Orders are Porter, Lector, Exorcist and Acolyte. The Major Orders are Subdeacon, Deacon and Priest. Priesthood also includes the Bishop, and all higher Church dignitaries. Every priest has received seven orders. The Sacrament of Holy Orders is as old as the Church.

"And Jesus coming, spoke to them, saying: All power is given to me in heaven and in earth. Going therefore, teach ye all nations; baptizing them in the name of the Father, and of the Son, and of the Holy Ghost. Teaching them to observe all things whatsoever I have commanded you." St. Matt. 28:18-20. "Do this for a commemoration of me." St. Luke 22:19. "Receive ye the Holy Ghost. Whose sins you shall forgive, they are forgiven them; and whose sins you shall retain, they are retained." St. John 20: 22, 23.

"And they chose Stephen, a man full of faith, and of the Holy Ghost, and Philip, and Prochorus, and Nicanor, and Timon, and Parmenas, and Nicolas, a proselyte of Antioch. These they set before the Apostles; and they praying, imposed hands upon them." Acts 6:5, 6.

Origen (died 255): "Dost thou think that they who exercise the ministry and glory in the order of the priesthood, walk according to their order and do all things which beseem that order? In like manner, deacons, do they walk according to the order of their ministry? Whence then is it that we often hear men blaspheme, and say, 'See what a bishop,' or, 'What a presbyter,' or, 'What a deacon?' Is not this said, when either a priest or a minister of God has dared to proceed in anywise contrary to the sacerdotal or Levitical order?" Homily 2 on Numbers.

The so-called *Apostolic Constitutions*, compiled about the year 400: "The bishop gives a blessing and does not receive it; he imposes hands, ordains, and offers sacrifice, he receives a blessing from the bishops, but never from priests. The bishop deposes every cleric that deserves deposition, except a bishop, for this he cannot do alone. The presbyter (priest) gives a blessing, and does not receive it: he receives a blessing from the bishop and from a fellow-priest, in like manner he blesses his fellow-priest; he imposes hands, but does not ordain; he deposes no one, but excommunicates those under him, if they deserve this punishment. The deacon does not give a blessing, but receives it from the bishop and the presbyter; he baptizes not, he offers not; but when the bishop or the presbyter offer, he distributes (communion) to the people, not indeed as a priest, but as minister of the priest." Book 8, Chap. 28.

St. Chrysostom (died 407): *"And they praying imposed hands upon them.* From this it is evident that they separated them from the multitude; and they bring them, the Apostles do not lead them. Observe how the writer avoids redundancy; for he does not say *how* they were ordained, but simply *that* they were *ordained by prayer*. Because *this* is the ordination. The hand is imposed upon a man, but God works all, and it is His hand that touches the head of him that is ordained, if he be ordained in a manner he ought to be." Commentary on Acts, Homily 14, No. 3.

St. Augustine (died 430): "When it is judged expedient for the Church, that such prelates on returning to the Catholic fellowship, should not exercise therein their honors, the sacraments themselves of ordination are not taken away from them, but remain with them." Against the Letter of Parmenianus, Book 2, Chap. 13, No. 28.

VII. Matrimony.

Matrimony is a sacrament which unites a Christian man and woman for life in lawful wedlock. God instituted it in Paradise (Gen. 1:28). Jesus raised it to the Sacrament of the Living.

Speaking of matrimony St. Paul writes: "This is a great sacrament; but I speak in Christ and in the Church." Eph. 5:32.

St. Epiphanius, Bishop of Salamis (died 403): "The same holy, Catholic, and apostolic Church has been wont to save also those who are in venerable wedlock. . . . Honorable therefore is marriage, seeing that He himself established it." Heresies, Bk. 1, P. 410.

St. Augustine (died 430): "Matrimony possesses a threefold good: fidelity, offspring, and the sacrament. Concerning fidelity it is required, that neither of the parties act in violation of the marriage ties; concerning the offspring, that it be received with love, nurtured with kindness, and educated piously; and concerning the sacrament, that the wedlock be not dissolved, and that neither, if divorced, be united to another." On Genesis, According to the Letter, Bk. 9, Chap. 7, No. 12. "Throughout all nations and men, the excellence of wedlock is in the procreation of children and in the faithfulness of chastity: but as regards the people of God, it is also in the holiness of the sacrament, through which holiness it is a crime, even for the party that is divorced, to marry another whilst the husband lives." De Bono Conjugali, No. 32.

"What, therefore, God hath joined together, let no man put asunder. Those that are well instructed in the Catholic Faith know that God has made marriage and that just as the union is from God, so divorce is from the devil. And for this reason, therefore, did the Lord being invited come to the wedding feast that He might confirm conjugal chastity and show forth the *Sacrament of Matrimony*." Tracts on St. John; Tract 9, 2.

St. Maximus, Bishop of Turin (died about 465): "The Son of God goes to the wedding feast that He may sanctify by the blessing of His presence what He had long before instituted by His power." Homily 23 (on Epiphany 7).

The Holy Sacrifice of the Mass

※※※

MALACHIAS, the last of the prophets, in the fifth century before Christ, delivered this message to the chosen people: "The son honoreth the father, and the servant his master: if then I be a father, where is my honor? And if I be a master, where is my fear? saith the Lord of hosts. To you, O priests, that despise my name, and have said: Wherein have we despised thy name? You offer polluted bread upon my altar, and you say: Wherein have we polluted thee? In that you say: The table of the Lord is contemptible. If you offer the blind for sacrifice, is it not evil? and if you offer the lame and the sick, is it not evil? offer it to thy prince, if he will be pleased with it, or if he will regard thy face, saith the Lord of hosts. And now beseech ye the face of God, that he may have mercy on you (for by your hand hath this been done), if by any means he will receive your faces, saith the Lord of hosts. Who is there among you, that will shut the doors and will kindle the fire on my altar gratis? I have no pleasure in you, saith the Lord of hosts; and I will not receive a gift of your hand. *For from the rising of the sun even to the going down, my name is great among the Gentiles, and in every place there is sacrifice, and there is offered to my name a clean oblation:* for my name is

The Catholic Church

great among the Gentiles, saith the Lord of hosts." Mal. 1:6-11.

In these words God announced through His prophet that the priesthood and the sacrifices of the Jews would be abolished, that He would not receive a gift of their hands, and that a new sacrifice would be offered in every place among all nations, from the east to the west, from the rising of the sun even to the going down, and that He will be pleased with this new sacrifice, the clean oblation. This sacrifice will not be confined to Juda's capital, nor the priesthood to the descendants of Aaron and Levi. His sacrifice as well as His priests will be among all nations, and on account of this His name is great among the Gentiles.

In vain do you look for the fulfillment of this prophecy, unless you turn your attention to the holy Sacrifice of the Mass. *The sacrifice of the Mass is the unbloody renewal of the bloody sacrifice of Calvary.* Under the appearance of bread and wine Jesus Christ offers Himself for us to His heavenly Father. The first holy Mass, however, preceded the bloody sacrifice of Calvary. Jesus Christ celebrated the first Mass at the Last Supper. The words of consecration which He made use of are still used by His priests. "Jesus took bread, and blessed, and broke: and gave to his disciples, and said: Take ye, and eat. *This is my body.* And taking the chalice, he gave thanks, and gave to them, saying: Drink ye all of this. *For this is my blood of the New Testament, which shall be shed for many unto remission of sins.*" St. Matt. 26:26-28.

That the Apostles exercised the power conferred

upon them, that they said Mass, may be seen from the first letter of St. Paul to the Corinthians, where he writes: "*The chalice of benediction, which we bless, is it not the communion of the blood of Christ? And the bread, which we break, is it not the partaking of the body of the Lord?*" 1 Cor. 10:16. The chalice containing the blood of Christ is blessed in Mass, and the species of bread is broken at Communion, the partaking of the body of the Lord.

For a sacrifice an altar is needed. St. Paul writes: "We have an altar, whereof they have no power to eat who serve the tabernacle." Heb. 13:10. The meaning of this sentence is: those who serve the tabernacle, i.e., who adhere to the Jewish rite, have no right to partake of the sacrifice of the New Law.

The *Didache* (meaning Doctrine or Teaching) is probably the oldest non-biblical writing of the Christian age. The unpretentious little treatise is certainly one of the most precious gems of ecclesiastical literature. It may be styled a Church Ritual; and, according to the best critics, it was written before the close of the first century most likely in Syria or Palestine. In the 14th chapter the author speaks of the Holy Sacrifice: "But on the day of the Lord assemble and break the Bread and give thanks,—after having confessed your faults, that your sacrifice may be a clean one. But let no one who has fallen out with his brother assemble with you before they are reconciled, that your sacrifice may not be desecrated; for this is the sacrifice of which the Lord has spoken: *In every place and at all times shall a clean oblation be offered to me; for I am a king, saith the Lord, and my name is wonderful amongst the Gentiles."*

St. Clement (died about 100): "They, therefore, that make their oblations at the appointed times, are acceptable and blessed, for those that follow the ordinances of the Lord, do not err." 1 Letter to the Corinthians, No. 40.

St. Ignatius (died 107): "Let no man deceive himself; unless a man be within the altar he stands deprived of the Bread of God." Letter to the Ephesians, No. 5.

St. Justin (died 167): "The oblation of wheaten flour, prescribed to be offered for those who were purified from leprosy, was a type of the bread of the Eucharist which our Lord Jesus commanded us to be offered as a commemoration of the passion which He endured for those who are purified from all iniquity, that we at the same time may give thanks to God, both for having made the world and all things in it for the sake of man, and for having delivered us from the wickedness in which we were; and for having overthrown principalities and powers, through Him, who, by the will of His Father, was made subject to suffering. Whence, God, as I said before, by Malachias, one of the twelve (minor prophets) declares of the sacrifices then offered by you: My will is not in you, saith the Lord; and I will not receive sacrifices from your hands: for, from the rising of the sun, even to the going down, my name hath been glorified among the Gentiles, and in every place incense is offered to my name, and a clean host, because my name is great among the Gentiles, saith the Lord. Even then does He foretell concerning the sacrifices offered unto Him, in every place by us Gentiles; that is of the Bread of the Eucharist and of the Cup in like manner of the Eucharist." Dialogue with the Jew Trypho, No. 41.

St. Irenaeus (died 202): "He took bread, which comes by creation, and gave thanks, saying: *This is my body*. And in like manner He confessed the cup, which is of this creation of ours, to be His own blood, and taught the new oblation of the New Testament, which (oblation) the Church, having received it from the Apostles, offers to God throughout the whole world, to Him who grants unto us sustenance,—the first fruits of His own gifts in the New Testament, respecting which Malachias, one of the twelve prophets, thus predicted: *I have no pleasure in you*, etc." Against Heresies, Book 4, Chap. 17, No. 5.

Tertullian (died 240): "We make oblations for the dead on their anniversaries instead of their birthdays." On the Crown, No. 3.

St. Cyprian of Carthage in Africa (d. 258): "If Christ Jesus our Lord and our God is Himself the Highpriest of God the Father, and offers Himself as a sacrifice to the Father, and commanded this to be done unto a commemoration of Him, then truly does that priest perform the functions of Christ who imitates what Christ did, and offers a true and full sacrifice to God in the Church." 63d Letter, No. 14.

St. Cyril of Jerusalem (386): "After the completion of the spiritual sacrifice of the Mass, after the completion of the unbloody worship, we pray to God over the oblation of propitiation for the general peace of the churches. We all pray and offer this sacrifice for every one who is in need of help. We remember those who have already gone before us, first the Patriarchs, the Prophets, the Apostles and the Martyrs, so that through their prayers and intercession God may look graciously upon our petitions; thereupon we pray for the deceased Holy Fathers and Bishops, and indeed for all our departed, since we believe that our prayers offered in the presence of this holy and worshipful sacrifice will be of the greatest utility to these souls. We offer up Christ slain for our sins to obtain pardon from the good God for them and for ourselves." Catechesis, 23:8-10.

St. Augustine (died 430): "Some communicate daily of the Body and Blood of Christ, others receive on certain days; elsewhere no day passes whereon the oblation is not made, whilst in other places on the Saturday and the Sunday only, in others on the Sunday only." 54th Letter (to Januarius), No. 2.

Thus we can adduce an abundance of testimonies from the writings of different Fathers of all nations and of the earliest centuries, that the Catholic Church, which encircles the globe, offered even then unto God this clean oblation in every place, from the east to the west, and without intermission. At this very moment the sun rises somewhere in the world, where the priests ascend the Altar to offer to God the holy Sacrifice of the Mass. The prophecy of Malachias is literally fulfilled in the Catholic Church.

Christian Denominations

QUESTIONS ON THE TEXT.

1. How would you prove the continuation of the American Republic?
2. Give a similar argument for the continuity of the Catholic Church.
3. What do we read in the Didache concerning Baptism?
4. Mention the names of eight Fathers of the Church, who wrote on Baptism.
5. Give the gist of their assertions.
6. What does Confirmation do to a baptized person?
7. Quote St. Innocent on Confirmation.
8. What is the Holy Eucharist?
9. In what words did Christ promise the Blessed Eucharist and how did He institute this Sacrament?
10. Quote St. Cyril of Jerusalem on the Blessed Eucharist.
11. What does St. Nilus write about the Blessed Eucharist?
12. What happens in the Sacrament of Penance?
13. Quote St. Ephraem on Confession.
14. How is Extreme Unction administered?
15. Quote St. Caesarius on Extreme Unction.
16. How many orders does a Priest receive?
17. In what words did Jesus give His Apostles and their successors the power to forgive sin? To consecrate? And to preach?
18. What does St. Paul write about Matrimony?
19. Explain what St. Augustine means by the threefold good of Matrimony.
20. Quote St. Maximus on Matrimony.
21. Give the prophecy of Malachias relative to the sacrifice of the Mass. How is it fulfilled?
22. Quote St. Ignatius on the sacrifice of the Mass.
23. How can you prove from a citation from Tertullian that Masses were said for the departed?
24. How often did the Catholics go to Holy Communion in the days of St. Augustine? Quote him in your answer.

The Blessed Virgin Mary

THE GREAT MOTHER OF GOD AND OUR DEAR MOTHER.

※※※

FOUR thousand years before "the fullness of time" had come, God announced the coming of the Blessed Virgin Mary. Speaking to the serpent that had seduced Eve, He says: "I will put enmities between thee and the woman, and thy seed and her seed: she shall crush thy head, and thou shalt lie in wait for her heel." Gen. 3: 15.

It cannot be denied that Almighty God and His archangel Gabriel and the Catholic Church have paid greater honor to the Blessed Virgin Mary, the Mother of God, than to any other saint.

Seven hundred years before her coming, God inspired His prophet Isaias to deliver this message: "Behold a virgin shall conceive, and bear a son, and his name shall be called Emmanuel." Is. 7:14. God exempted her from the stain of original sin. The Son of God called her by the endearing title of mother. The Holy Ghost overshadowed her and filled her with grace.

Whenever an angel appeared to announce some divine message, he inspired the listener with awe and worded his sentences in an authoritative form as a superior speaking to an inferior. But when the archangel Gabriel came to announce unto Mary that God had chosen her to be His mother, he greeted her in the name of God, praised her sanctity, her relation to the Lord, and her singular blessedness among women. His words clearly indicate that he considered her superior to himself.

Imitating the example set by God and His archangel, the Catholic Church venerates the Blessed Virgin Mary in a special manner. As God commanded His archangel to do, so every true Catholic does repeatedly during the day: he greets the Blessed Virgin Mary: "Hail, full of grace, the Lord is with thee: blessed art thou among women." St. Luke 1:28. As the Son of God called her His mother, so the Catholic Church calls her the Mother of God. As the Holy Ghost overshadowed her and filled her with grace, so the Catholic Church exalts her; and with great solemnity annually celebrates in her honor a number of beautiful feasts. Who can reasonably blame the Church for honoring her, whom God so highly honored? What Christian will dare to rebuke that Christian who dearly loves the mother of Christ? Who can find anything objectionable in the title "Mother of God," if he believes that her Son is God? Why should anybody be afraid to do what God does? what His Church always did and still does? I, for one, feel happy that the Blessed Virgin Mary is really the Mother of God; and gladly do I confess my heartfelt love for her, proclaiming that I love the Blessed Virgin Mary, the Mother of God, more than I love any other creature, and I hope to live and die with my heart aflame with love for her, whom Jesus called His dear mother.

"And Mary said: My soul doth magnify the Lord. And my spirit hath rejoiced in God my Savior. Because he hath regarded the humility of his handmaid; for behold from henceforth all generations shall call me blessed." St. Luke 1:46-48.

This prophecy which she uttered in the presence of her cousin Elisabeth is literally fulfilled; all generations call her blessed. A few quotations culled from patristic literature may help to convince my readers of this fact.

St. Irenaeus (died about 202): "As Eve, through the discourse of a fallen angel, was seduced so as to flee from God, acting contrary to His word; so also it was announced to Mary through the message of a (good) angel that she was to bear God, being obedient to His Word. And as Eve disobeyed God, so Mary was persuaded to obey God, that the virgin Mary might become the advocate of the virgin Eve. And as the human race was delivered over through a virgin, so it is saved through a virgin." Against Heresies, Bk. 5, Chap. 19.

Of all the many encomiums on the Blessed Virgin the most tender, the most touching, the most exquisitely beautiful are those so lavishly scattered over the works of the soulful poet of far away Syria, *St. Ephraem*, who flourished toward the end of the fourth century. Here is one of these passages: "Thou and Thy Mother are the only ones, who are in every way perfectly beautiful, for in Thee, O Lord, there is no stain; no stain also in Thy Mother." From "Songs of Nisibis," No. 27.

St. Gregory of Nazianzus (died about 390): "Saying this and still more (prayers addressed to God, the deliverer from all dangers and evil), she (Justina) suppliantly *implores the Virgin Mary* to aid a virgin in danger, and fortifies herself with the medicine of fasting and of prostration on the earth." Sermon on St. Cyprian of Antioch, No. 11.

St. Epiphanius (d. 403): "I hear that some one is devising some folly regarding the holy and ever-virgin Mary, and dares to speak ill of her. . . . Whence this wicked temper? Whence this great audacity? Does not her very name bear witness against and convince thee, thou contentious man? Who ever, or what age ever presumed to utter the name of Mary the holy and, when asked, has not instantly added in reply,—'the Virgin?' . . . And to holy Mary is added the epithet, 'the Virgin,' and this shall never be altered. For she the holy ever remained spotless. Does not nature itself instruct thee? Oh, the unheard of madness! oh, sad novelty! . . . How dare they attack the spotless Virgin; she who was found worthy to be the dwelling place of the Son; she who was, for this very reason, chosen from among the thousands of Israel to be the vessel, and the alone memorable dwelling place of the (divine) birth. . . . From that Eve the whole human race on earth has been derived. But, truly, from Mary life itself was born into this world, that she might bring forth Him that liveth, and become the mother of the living. . . . Whosoever honors the mother, honors His saint, too; and whoso puts dishonor on a saint, puts dishonor on his own Lord.... Let Mary be in honor; but let the Father, the Son, and the Holy Ghost be adored." Panarian, or, as it is frequently quoted, Heresies, Bk. 3, No. 78.

St. Ambrose (d. 397): "Oh, the riches of Mary's virginity! Like a cloud she rained upon the earth the grace of Christ; for concerning her was it written: *'Behold the Lord cometh sitting upon a light cloud,'* truly *light*, she who knew not the burdens of wedlock; truly *light*, she who relieved this world from the heavy debt of sins. *Light* she was who bore in her womb the remission of sins." On the Training of a Virgin, Chap. 13.

St. Cyril, Patriarch of Alexandria (d. 444), at the Council of Ephesus, 431, delivered several panegyrics on the Blessed Virgin, from one of which I quote: "Hail, holy Trinity, who hast called us together into this church of Mary, the Mother of God. Hail, Mary, mother of God, venerable treasury of the whole world; inextinguishable lamp; crown of God, virginity, scepter of orthodoxy; indestructible temple; repository of the Illimitable; mother and virgin, through whom He who cometh in the name of the Lord is called blessed in the holy Gospel. Hail, thou who didst contain the Illimitable in thy hallowed womb; through whom the Trinity is blessed; through whom the precious cross is celebrated and venerated throughout the whole world; through whom angels and archangels are filled with gladness; through whom heaven exults; through whom demons are put to flight; through whom the tempter-devil fell from heaven; through whom every creature, swayed by the idol of madness, has come to the knowledge of the truth; through whom holy baptism is the portion of believers; through whom is the oil of gladness; through whom the churches have been built over the whole world; through whom the nations are brought unto penitence; and why multiply words? Through whom the only-begotten Son of God shone forth, *a light to those that sat in darkness and in the shadow of death*. Through whom prophets predicted; through whom Apostles proclaimed salvation to the nations; through whom the dead were raised; through whom kings reign; through the Holy Trinity. And who amongst men is able to proclaim (worthily) the thrice-glorious Mary! ... Be it ours to worship the undivided Trinity, hymning the praises of Mary, ever Virgin." Homily at Ephesus, P. 355-358.

In the 39th sermon found amongst the works of St. Gregory Thaumaturgus, *St. Basil of Seleucia* calls her, "The Holy Virgin and Mother of God;" "Hail, full of grace, who dost mediate between God and man," "O all holy Virgin, of whom whosoever utters all that is venerable and glorious, errs not against the truth," etc. Parisian Edition of the Works of St. Gregory Thaumaturgus, Orat. 39, Pages 205, 211, etc.

Theodotus, Bishop of Ancyra, who died before 446, in his sermon on the Mother of God and Simeon thus paraphrases the angelic salutation: "Hail thou perfume-breathing name; hail, thou most bright and lovely being; hail, most venerable memorial; hail, salutary and spiritual fleece; hail, clothed with light, mother of a brightness that knows no setting; hail, spotless mother of holiness; hail, most pellucid spring of life-giving waters, etc." Gallandis Edition, Vol. 9, No. 3, P. 460.

St. Peter Chrysologus institutes a contrast between Eve and the Blessed Virgin Mary: "It was Christ's will that as through Eve death came to all men, so through Mary life might return to all." Serm. 99.

As the author of the book, "Faith of Catholics," aptly remarks, concerning *St. Proclus* (died 446), "The addresses, to the Blessed Virgin, of this patriarch of Constantinople, would fill a goodly pamphlet." I subjoin one of his extracts. "The holy mother of God, the Virgin Mary, has, on this occasion called us here together; she that spotless treasury of virginity; that spiritual paradise of the second Adam, the virgin and heaven, God's only bridge to men." Vol.3, P. 404.

Volumes upon volumes might be filled with extracts from the works of able and saintly writers of the past and present to show that from century to century the world over the Catholic Church has chanted and still proclaims the praises of the Mother of God and greatly relies upon her maternal protection. Two entire months of the year, May and October, are in a special manner dedicated to the veneration of the Blessed Virgin Mary. Thousands of churches are dedicated to her; a great number of confraternities bestow well-deserved extraordinary honor upon her; institutions of charity flourish under her special protection; and every practical Catholic greets her repeatedly during the day in the words of the archangel Gabriel: "Hail (Mary) full of grace, the Lord is with thee," etc. What our dear heavenly Mother predicted, is always fulfilled in the Catholic Church: all generations call her blessed. Experience and observation bear witness to the fact that the Mother of God takes a maternal interest in our welfare. The more we love and venerate the Blessed Virgin Mary, the better will we adore God and keep His commandments.

He who sincerely loves Jesus Christ will also respect and venerate His dear immaculate mother. He who believes that Christ is God, must call His mother, the Mother of God. And whosoever denies to the Blessed Virgin Mary the title of Mother of God, denies the divinity of her Son. Jesus is God. Mary, His mother, is the Mother of God.

A Brief Synopsis of Catholic Doctrine

⇶

THERE is but one God in three distinct persons, Father, Son, and Holy Ghost. These three divine persons have one and the same divine nature. We call this the mystery of the Blessed Trinity.

The second person of the Blessed Trinity, the Son of God, became man, assumed His human nature from the Blessed Virgin Mary, of whom He was born into this world over nineteen hundred years ago. He is the promised Redeemer whom the prophets foretold, the Savior of the world. He enlightened the world which was sitting in darkness and in the shadow of death in consequence of the sin of disobedience of our first parents, original sin; and He finally died on the cross to save mankind from eternal death and to re-open heaven for us. He amply provided for the needs of every individual soul and deposited His means of salvation in the Church which He founded. He ascended into heaven and sent the Holy Ghost upon His Apostles, and He will come again at the end of the world to judge the living and the dead. He who redeemed the world will also judge it.

God created man to His own image and likeness, endowing him with reason, free will, and immortality. The human soul will live for ever. Death, the separation of the soul from the body, came into the world through original sin. The Son of God,—who as the Son of the Blessed Virgin is called Jesus Christ,—atoned for this sin and all actual sins. Since Jesus Christ died for all, every one may be saved, if he co-operates to the best of his ability with the grace, which God gives to every one. No one is created for hell; everyone is created for heaven. But heaven is a reward. We have a free will; we can choose to do the good or the evil. We will be judged according to the use and abuse of our reason and free will.

To help us and to guard us, God has given unto every one an angel, a ministering spirit, whom we call guardian angel. These angels belong to the world of spirits which God created in the beginning and are of the number of those who remained faithful to God at the time when Lucifer and his angels rebelled against Him. The rebellious angels were hurled into hell, the place of everlasting punishment, created for the abode of the fallen spirits.

At the moment of death, the soul of man appears before God to be judged according to her thoughts deliberately entertained, her words consciously uttered, her wilful deeds and voluntary omissions of duty as well as her acts of heroic virtue. God is just. Those who die in the state of mortal sin are lost and sentenced to hell; but those who die in the state of sanctifying grace, will enter the eternal joys of heaven. If, however, the soul is not entirely free from all defilement, such as smaller imperfections, venial sins, or temporal punishment due to sin, the soul will be purged of these defilements and thus be prepared to enter heaven. This state and place of purgation we call purgatory. The souls detained in it, we call the Poor Souls. We can be of some help to them in coming to God, by praying for them, by offering up indulgences for them (an indulgence is a remission of temporal punishment due to sin), by giving alms or performing other acts of charity, and above all by having Masses said for them. We are in a position to help the Poor Souls. We believe in the Communion of Saints, i.e., in the union which exists between the Church Triumphant in heaven, the Church Militant on earth, and the Church Suffering in Purgatory. All loyal Catholics belong to the Church Militant. Whilst we extend one hand to help the Poor Souls, the members of the Church Suffering, we raise the other in supplication to the Angels and Saints, to the members of the Church Triumphant in Heaven.

The angels and saints of heaven are forever infinitely happy with God. All their wishes are fulfilled, and none of their requests will ever be denied. God listens to their prayers. They can and do pray for us. We pray to them that they may intercede for us with God. We venerate them as friends of God. But more than any other saint do we venerate, love, and invoke the Mother of Jesus Christ, the ever Blessed Virgin Mary, who was never tainted with sin; for she was conceived and born without sin; and lived and died without ever committing any imperfection that would attain to the nature of a sin.

As a dutiful child naturally esteems and venerates the heirlooms and portraits of his departed parents, so we pay honor and respect to the relics and pictures of the saints. This honor reflects upon the saint, the friend of God, and redounds to our spiritual benefit; for it inspires us with the heroism necessary to imitate the exalted example of the saints in serving God. It is thus a means of sanctification.

Other, more essential, means of sanctification are the sacraments as has already been mentioned. Jesus Christ instituted seven sacraments. Without baptism no other sacrament can be validly received. Through baptism all sins are effaced, original and actual, or personal, sins. Mortal sins committed after baptism are forgiven in the sacrament of Penance to those who are sincerely contrite and humbly confess their sins to a priest who is authorized to absolve in the name of God. In Holy Communion Jesus comes to us under the appearance of bread. In Holy Mass He offers Himself in our behalf to His heavenly Father.

His representative as head of the Church is the Holy Father, the Pope, who is infallible whenever as head and teacher of the whole Church he speaks ex cathedra in matters of doctrine or morals. Infallibility does not mean impeccability; that is, it does not mean that the Pope cannot sin. He, like any other human being, has a free will and must use it for the good, if he wants to enter life everlasting. His position as head of the Church is in no way a guarantee of his salvation; but it is a guarantee of the infallibility of his decision in decreeing what the Church is to believe as revealed. Infallibility does not mean that the Pope can invent some new doctrine, but it means that he can designate infallibly the teaching which the Church has always held, and point out and anathematize heretical innovations. The Catholic Church is infallible; for it is under the guidance of the Holy Ghost. The gates of hell shall never prevail against it. It is infallible in its teachings and means of salvation.

THE CATHOLIC CHURCH IS THE TRUE CHURCH.

In the preceding chapters we have seen that the Church which Jesus Christ founded and to which He promised that the gates of hell shall not prevail against it continued throughout all the centuries of the Christian era; it still exists. This true Church is no other than the Catholic Church. The Catholic Church alone claims and proves theologically and historically that it is the only Church which Jesus Christ founded: it alone dates back to *Him*.

Spread over the whole world this Church of which God is the founder has at present over four hundred million members. Though, like unto its divine founder, persecuted from the beginning, hated by all the enemies of the cross, the Catholic Church continues to flourish in its noble and sublime mission of saving immortal souls. It is for ever the mightiest bulwark against the wild and destructive forces in social life, the defender of virtue and justice, and the mother of numberless heroic saints, whose sanctity

God attested by astounding miracles. During the last nineteen centuries the Catholic Church has witnessed the rise and the fall of many a nation. Kingdoms and republics that antagonized the Church and stood at the zenith of their glory boasting of their tyranny over the Catholic Church have sunk to the nadir of misery. They have passed into oblivion; but the Catholic Church is still there and as glorious today as it was at any time. There is no doubt that it will continue its noble work of saving souls, even the souls of its present enemies. To save even its bitterest enemies from eternal damnation, to forgive in order to gain them for heaven: this is the attitude of the Catholic Church towards those who are blinded by prejudice against it. Akin to the conduct of Jesus Christ towards His enemies is the attitude of the Catholic Church towards its persecutors. "Father forgive them, for they know not what they do." Jesus Christ is the strength of the Catholic Church, the center of its devotions, the magnet of its heroism, the cause of its many saints, and the reason of its stability. "Behold I am with you all days, even to the consummation of the world." Jesus dwells in the Catholic Church in the Sacrament of the Altar. The Holy Ghost abides with the Church and guards it against all error in doctrine.

To belong to the Catholic Church means to be a member of the Church of which the God-man Jesus Christ is the founder: it means to be a member of the one and only true Church. This is the Catholic Church which Jesus founded upon His Apostles, of which St. Peter was appointed by Him the first head: "To thee I will give the keys of the kingdom of heaven." "Thou art Peter, and upon this rock I will build my Church, and the gates of hell shall not prevail against it." "Feed my lambs, feed my sheep." This is the Church which the Apostles spread the world over; which exists since the time of Christ as Christ established it. It has His teachings today as He gave them to His Church. It has the legitimate successor of St. Peter in the person of the Bishop of Rome, the head of the whole Church. It is Catholic, that is universal, as to time and place: it exists without any break or interruption since the time of Christ; it is found the world over, everywhere teaching the same doctrines, everywhere using the same seven Sacraments, everywhere offering up to God the same adorable sacrifice of the Mass, everywhere acknowledging the same supreme head of the Church, our Holy Father, the Pope. It is Catholic, for it is for the salvation of all mankind. Whosoever honestly and sincerely strives to become a member of the Church, no matter how poor or how rich, no matter what his nationality may be, he or she will be admitted into the Church. The Church bars no one from membership who seeks to save his soul in the manner ordained by God.

If perchance you, kind reader, should wish to be received into the Church, all you have to do is to call on the Catholic Priest and tell him that you desire to become a Catholic. He will tell you what to do, and with God's grace you will be a Catholic some day, and as such experience that real happiness, peace of conscience, and security of soul can be found in the Catholic Church, for it is a divine institution with Jesus dwelling in it.

According to the Catholic World Atlas published upon the command of Pope Pius XI, we find that there are in

all Europe	208,881,598
all America	199,096,603
all Asia	16,535,812
all Africa	5,329,455
Australia & Islands	1,584,541
Total Catholics	431,428,009

Questions on the Text.

1. Which is the first revelation of God that refers to the Blessed Virgin?
2. Prove that God honors the Blessed Virgin in a special manner.
3. How did the Archangel Gabriel honor the Blessed Virgin Mary?
4. What honor does the Catholic Church bestow upon her?
5. Why do we call Blessed Virgin the Mother of God?
6. What has St. Irenaeus to say about the Mother of God?
7. Who calls her the venerable treasure of the whole world?
8. Give a citation from St. Ephraem on the Mother of God.
9. How many persons are there in God?
10. How many natures are there in the Blessed Trinity?
11. Why did the Son of God become man?
12. Mention the three great prerogatives of the human soul, where-with God endowed it.
13. If every human being receives sufficient grace to be saved, how then do you account for it that some are lost?

The Catholic Church

14. In what state must the soul be at the hour of death to go immediately into Heaven?
15. What is Purgatory?
16. What is Hell?
17. What do you understand by the Communion of Saints?
18. What is the state of the angels and saints in Heaven?
19. The veneration of relics and pictures of Saints reflects honor upon whom?
20. When is the Pope infallible?
21. Briefly prove that the Catholic Church is the true Church founded by our Lord Jesus Christ.
22. What does it mean to belong to the Catholic Church?
23. How many Catholics are there at present?

The Greek Orthodox Church

IN the year 867 Photius, Patriarch of Constantinople by intrusion, caused a temporary schism between the Eastern and Western Church. He had received orders at the hands of Gregory Asbestas, an excommunicated bishop. St. Ignatius, the legitimate Patriarch, was dragged from prison to prison and cruelly persecuted by the intruder. The Council of Constantinople, 869, deposed and excommunicated Photius and declared Ignatius the lawful Patriarch of Constantinople. Three days after the death of St. Ignatius the excommunicated Photius, who had ingratiated himself with the emperor, was reinstated in the see of Constantinople. After this he was repeatedly excommunicated.

"The schism, for a time extinguished, was revived in 1043 by the haughty and ignorant Caerularius, Patriarch of Constantinople, who added a few ridiculous accusations to the more weighty charges of Photius. At the request of Emperor Constantine IX., Pope St. Leo IX. sent three legates to Constantinople with a written refutation of the charges of Caerularius. The Patriarch and his party refused all communication with the legates, forbade them to celebrate Mass, and displayed so much hostility to the plan of union proposed by the Emperor, that on the 16th of July, 1054, the legates laid the document of the

The Greek Orthodox Church 113

Patriarch's excommunication upon the high altar of St. Sophia's Church and left Constantinople. All further efforts of union, even the deposition and banishment of Caerularius, failed to effect a permanent reunion. The haughty Patriarch and his party had succeeded in filling the minds of the populace with a blind hatred of the Western Church. The other Patriarchates of the East remained in union with the Holy See till the twelfth century, when they were gradually drawn into the schism. The Russian Church shared the fate of the Patriarchate of Constantinople, to which she was immediately subjected. But so imperceptibly did the schism enter Russia that their ritual books retain to the present day a series of prayers which express the faith in the Primacy of the Roman See in the fullest sense. It was only when the Greek Nicephorus became Metropolitan of Kief, that the Byzantine hatred of Rome was instilled into the Russian Church. But it was then too late to change the form of the liturgical books sanctioned by immemorial use." Guggenberger, General History of the Christian Era, Vol. I, Page 290.

Therefore the Greek Church, as a separate body, dates back to the eleventh century. It refused to obey the Church. It does not acknowledge the authority nor heed the voice of the shepherd, whom Christ commissioned to feed the lambs and the sheep. "If he will not hear the Church, let him be to thee as the heathen and publican." Matt. 18:17.

It is generally known that the chain is no stronger than its weakest link; break one of the links and the chain is broken altogether. By violently tearing themselves away from the supreme jurisdiction of the Pope the schismatics tore the chain which held them to the Church which Jesus built upon St. Peter: "Thou art Peter; and upon this rock I will build my church, and the gates of hell shall not prevail against it." St. Matt. 16:18.

Not all Greeks belong to the Greek Church. Many of them are true and devout members of the Catholic Church. These we call United Greeks, or simply Catholics. Those belonging to the Greek Church are called schismatics, because they separated from the true Church. They claim 127,541,718 members.

The Lutheran Church

※※※

BY this title we designate the followers of Luther, a priest and monk, who fell away from the Catholic Church and started a new sect in 1520, the same year in which he was excommunicated. Lutherans, however, prefer to date their church back to October 31, 1517, the day on which Luther publicly affixed his notorious ninety-five theses to the doors of the castle church of Wittenberg.

In any case, even the Lutherans admit that the church which Luther founded differs from the existing Catholic Church. The Lutheran Church is fifteen hundred years too late to be the Church which Jesus Christ founded; for Jesus lived fifteen hundred years before the rise and spread of Lutheranism. Its very name designates it as a human institution, and history proves that it is nothing more. Luther is its founder; his followers are called Lutherans. They number about 50,000,000.

In the wake of Luther's so-called reformation came rebellion, bloodshed and licentiousness. No true historian can ever cheat himself into the conviction that Protestantism brought peace and happiness. On the contrary, it is an undeniable historical fact that Luther by his incentive talk and venomous pen, particularly by publishing his treatise on Christian Liberty, destroyed peace and harmony throughout the Fatherland and caused the riotous and atrocious, most bloody revolt of 1525, known as the Peasant War. During the carnage of the war Luther took the escaped nun Catherine of Bora for his wife.

When the lawful princes were about to crush the rebellion and to protect themselves against the ever increasing fury of the mob, Luther turned against the peasants and urged the princes to dire revenge. "Prick, strike, strangle! Slay front and rear, nothing is more devilish than sedition, etc." Such was Luther's advice, which undoubtedly contributed to the slaughter of the deluded peasants.

Behold the dismal sight conjured by an apostate, a sinful, insubordinate, excommunicated man, the Father of Protestantism! Over one thousand castles and convents were plundered, demolished and turned into ghastly ruins. Hundreds of hamlets were burnt to the ground. Thousands of defenseless people, relatives even, were mutilated and most cruelly tortured by the disciples of misnamed religious tolerance. The land lay waste, whilst the homeless widows and orphans of more than one hundred and fifty thousand slain peasants went to strange villages asking for a morsel of food. Where formerly people had lived peacefully together, there rebellion and hatred entered, and despotism ruled with an iron hand. This universal curse of discord, devastation and despicable barbarism was the result of revolt against the Church. The pretentious cry for reformation and freedom of conscience; the plea of protesting against the Church, cannot efface the real names: rebellion and intoler-

The Lutheran Church

ance. Listen to what St. Paul says: "Now I beseech you, brethren, to mark them who make dissensions and offences contrary to the doctrine which you have learned, and avoid them. For they that are such, serve not Christ our Lord, but their own belly; and by pleasing speeches and good words, seduce the hearts of the innocent." Rom. 16:17, 18.

Contrary to the doctrine of the Church, Luther denied the existence of purgatory and the utility of praying for the dead; he abolished the invocation of saints; denied the indissolubility of marriage; and granted permission to the Landgrave of Hesse to marry a second wife and ridiculed and renounced four of the seven Sacraments, retaining only Baptism, Holy Eucharist, and Penance. Because his rank heresy of the justification of faith alone was diametrically opposed to what St. James asserts in his Epistle, Luther would not even bend his stubborn neck to an inspired writer, but rejected that Epistle and blasphemously called it an epistle of straw.

The different Evangelical Lutheran churches that have sprung up, or seceded so numerously since the time of Luther, agree in their interpretation of the Apostles' Creed, the Nicene Creed, the Athanasian Creed, and the Augsburg Confession. Though none of the Lutheran ministers has any valid ordination from his church, though none of them can really consecrate, nevertheless the stricter Lutherans believe in the real presence of Jesus Christ. They teach that Jesus Christ is present by assuming the nature of bread and wine. In this they are mistaken. For if

Christ would assume the nature of bread and wine, there would be four natures in Christ, namely, the divine, the human, the breaden and that of the wine. There are only two natures in Christ, the divine and the human. The Lutherans differ with the Catholic Church in holding that the bread remains and Christ is in the bread; whereas the Catholic Church teaches, what Jesus plainly said: "This is my body," the bread and wine are changed into the body and blood of Jesus Christ. So much is certain, when a Lutheran minister attempts to consecrate, the bread remains bread only, as it was before; but when a Catholic Priest consecrates at Mass, the bread and wine are substantially changed into the body and blood of Jesus Christ. Lutherans have no Sacrament of Holy Orders. Without it, there is no consecration. In some of their teachings and in many of their practices the Lutherans are similar to the Catholics, for they have retained many of the good things which Luther took along from the Catholic Church. The Bible is one of these things. Would to God that they had retained it, correct and complete, as they got it from the Church.

Denying the efficacy of sacramental confession, they pin their hope of salvation to faith alone. Jesus said to His disciples and their legitimate successors: "Whose sins you shall forgive, they are forgiven them; and whose sins you shall retain, they are retained." St. John 20:23. Entangled in the meshes of falsehood, it is hard for them to extricate themselves from the tightly woven net of prejudice and to behold and to love the Church which Jesus founded about 1500 years before the birth of Lutheranism.

The strict German Lutherans of today are, as a rule, honest and moral people. They have their parochial schools and make great sacrifices for the maintenance of the same. When once converted to the Church, they make very good Catholics. May God give this grace of conversion to many of them!

A Few Remarks About the German Translation of the Bible.

With many Protestants, especially Lutherans, the erroneous opinion prevails that Luther was the first who translated the Holy Bible into the German language. A number of complete German Bibles were printed about the year 1460. Luther was born in 1483. We cannot presume that he made any translations before his birth, neither in his infancy.

On January 27, 1912, I spent some profitable hours in the valuable library of St. Benedict's Abbey, Atchison, Kansas, and there I saw and partly read a German Bible, which was printed on St. Urban's day, 1487, when Luther was but a mere child. Another Bible in the German language which antedates Luther's translation may be seen in the University of Notre Dame, Indiana. It is the second volume of a Bible printed in March, 1483, about seven months before the birth of Martin Luther. The place of publication was Nuerenberg, and the printer was the famous Anthony Koburger.

Luther did not give the Bible to the people. They had the Bible long before he was born.

"Whereas the university at Erfurt contained an eight years' course of the study of Holy Scripture, he (Luther) seems to have ignored it entirely, giving all his attention to profane letters. Thus it may well be that, when later on he took to the reading of the Holy Bible, he found this precious treasure almost a new book to him, though it had been the most familiar of all books during the preceding centuries. So there are today thousands of Christian literateurs and scientists who have never read the Holy Gospels. The late historian, Joannes Janssen, in his monumental work, 'The History of the German People,' has forever dispelled the mist that used to surround the life of Luther with a halo of glory...." Coppens' The Protestant Reformation, Pages 16, 17.

King Henry VIII. of England Against Martin Luther.

Whilst Martin Luther hurled his unqualified slurs and calumnies against the Catholic Church and the Pope and ridiculed most of the seven Sacraments, Henry VIII., King of England, having improved his natural talents by an education which was intended to prepare him for the Archbishopric of Canterbury, wrote his excellent work, "Defence of the Seven Sacraments," against Luther. He exposed Luther's many fallacies and called him a prevaricator, a corrupter of the Testament, a labyrinth of stupidity, a destroyer of both soul and body, a little know-it-all, and a pest to be avoided. Upon the receipt of this book Pope Leo X. bestowed upon Henry VIII. the title, "Defender

The Lutheran Church

of the Faith;" which title the rulers of England bear to this day. King Henry defended with heart and soul the independence of the Holy See until the Pope had to forbid him to unjustly put aside his lawful wife, Queen Catherine, in order to marry Anne Boleyn. Goaded on by his unbridled sensuality and encouraged by his many sycophants, King Henry tore away from the Church and became its bloodthirsty persecutor.

In spite of his later crimes his "Defence of the Seven Sacraments" was not altered by him. We still possess it as he sent it to the Holy Father. Since it was written at Luther's time it undoubtedly furnishes some valuable and interesting information.

"Let us therefore begin where he began himself, with the adorable Sacrament of Christ's Body. The changing of the name thereof, calling it 'The Sacrament of Bread,' shows that this man cannot well endure, that we should be put in mind of Christ's Body, by the name of the *Blessed Sacrament*; and that, if under any fair pretext, it were possible for him, he would give it a worse name. How much differs the judgment of St. Ambrose from this man's, when he says, *Though the form of bread and wine is seen upon the altar, yet we must believe that there is nothing else but the Body and Blood of Christ*; by which words it clearly appears that St. Ambrose confesses no other substance to remain with the Body and Blood of Christ in the Sacrament, when he says, *That which is seen under the form of bread and wine, is nothing else but the Body and Blood of Christ*. If St. Ambrose had only said Flesh and Blood, without adding anything more, perhaps Luther would have said that the bread and wine were there also; as Luther himself says, That the substance of the Flesh is with the bread, and the substance of the Blood along with the wine; but seeing St. Ambrose says, *That there is nothing else but the Flesh and Blood*, it appears that he is manifestly against Luther, who affirms that the bread is with the Flesh, and the wine with the Blood.

"And though this which Luther says were as true as it is false viz., that the bread should remain mingled with the body of Christ; yet was it not necessary for him to blot the name of the *Body of Christ* out of the Sacrament, in which he confesses that the true Body of Christ is." Defence of the Seven Sacraments, Pages 212, 214.

"In the meanwhile, let us truly examine how subtlely, under pretense of favoring the laity, he endeavors to stir them up to a hatred against the clergy; for when he resolved to render the Church's Faith suspicious, that its authority should be of no consequence against him (and so by opening that gap, he might destroy the chiefest mysteries of Christianity), he began with that thing, which he foresaw would be praised and applauded by the people. For he touched the old sore by which Bohemia had been formerly blistered, viz., that the laity ought to receive the Eucharist under both kinds. When first he began to handle this point, he only said that the Pope would do well to have it ordained by a general council that the laity should receive the Sacrament under both kinds; but that being by some disputed with him, and denied, he was not contented to stop there, but grew to such a perverse height that he condemned the whole clergy of wickedness for not doing it without staying for any council. For my part, I do not dispute the first; and though to me no reasons appear why the Church should not ordain, that the Sacrament should be administered to the laity under both kinds; yet doubt I not but what was done in times past, by omitting it, and also in hindering it to be so administered now, is very convenient. Nor can I believe that the whole clergy (during so many ages) have been so void of sense as to incur eternal punishment for a thing by which they could reap no temporal good. It further appears not to be a thing of such danger, because God not only bestowed heaven upon these men who did this thing themselves, and writ that it ought to be done, but likewise would have them honored on earth by those by whom He is adored Himself. Amongst whom (to omit others) was that most learned and holy man Thomas Aquinas, whom I do more willingly name here, because the wickedness of Luther cannot endure the sanctity of this man, but reviles with his foul lips him whom all Christians honor. There are very many, though not canonized, who are contrary to Luther's opinion in this, and to whom, in piety and learning, Luther is no wise comparable: among whom was the Master of the Sentences, Nicholas de Lyra, and many others; to each of whom it behooves all Christians to give more credit than to Luther.

"But pray, observe how Luther staggers, and contradicts himself: in one place he says that Christ in his Last Supper not only said to all the faithful as permitting, but as commanding, 'Drink ye all of this'; yet afterwards (fearing to offend the laity whom he flatters, with a view to stir up hatred against the priests), he adds these words, not that they who use but one kind do sin against Christ, but left it to every man's discretion, saying: 'As often as you do this, do it in remembrance of me'; but, says he, they sin who forbid to give both kinds to such as are willing to receive them; the blame, says he, lies on the clergy and not on the laity. You see how clearly he first holds it for a command, and then says it is no commandment, but a thing left to every man's discretion. What need we contradict him, who so often contradicts himself?" Pages 214, 216, 218.

"This worse than sacrilegious caitiff endeavors to scatter abroad the Church's most splendid congregation; to extinguish its pillar of fire; to violate the ark of the covenant, and to destroy *the chief and only sacrifice which reconciles us to God*, and which is always offered for the sins of the people; for as much as in him lies, he robs the Mass of the benefits that flow from it to the people, denying it to be a good work, or to bring to them any kind of profit. In which thing I know not whether more to admire his wickedness or his foolish hope, or rather his mad pride; who, seeing so many obstructions before him, as he himself mentions, brings nothing with him whereby to remove the least, but seems as if he would go about to pierce a rock with a reed. For he sees, and confesses himself, that the opinions of the Holy Fathers are against him, as also the Canon of the Mass, with the custom of the universal Church, confirmed by the usage of so many ages, and the consent of so many people." Defence of Seven Sacraments, Page 254.

"Luther so much commends faith to us as not only to permit us to abstain from good works, but also encourages us to commit any kind of action, how bad soever: 'For (says he) you see now how rich the baptized man is, who cannot lose his salvation, though willing to do it, by any sin whatsoever, except infidelity; for no sins can damn him, but only incredulity.' O most impious doctrine, and mistress of all impiety! so hateful in itself to pious ears, that there is no need to confute it: adultery will not damn them! Murder will not damn! Perjury will not damn! Is not parricide damnable either, if every one believe that he shall be saved, through the virtue of the promise alone in baptism? For this he openly asserts; nor do the words, which he presently adds, correct his sentence in any wise, but rather add to the force of it. For he saith, 'That all things, if faith return, or stand in the divine promise made by the baptized, are swallowed up in a moment in the same faith; rather by the faith of God, for he cannot deny himself, if you confess him, and stick faithfully to his promise.' By these words, what else does he say but what he has said before, that, 'Infidelity excepted, all other crimes are in a moment swallowed up by faith alone; if you confess Christ, and stick faithfully to his promise'; that is, if you firmly believe that you are to be saved by faith, whatsoever you do notwithstanding. And that you may the less doubt what he aims at, 'Contrition (says he) and confession of sins, as also satisfaction, and all these human inventions, will forsake you, and leave you the more unhappy; if you buy yourselves with them forgetting this divine truth.' What truth, pray? 'This that no sins can damn thee, but infidelity only.' What Christian ears can with patience hear the pestilentious hissing of this serpent, by which he extols baptism, for no other end but to depress penance and establish the grace of baptism for free liberty of sinning? Contrary to what is that sentence of St. Hierom, which says that *Penance is the plank after ship-wreck*. But this agrees not with Luther, for he denies sin to be the ship-wreck of faith, and disputes it, as if that only word should totally destroy all the strength of faith. But beside Luther, who is ignorant that a sinner not only is not saved by the only faith of baptism, but also that the baptism will add to his damnation? And indeed deservedly, because he has offended God, from whom he had the whole grace of baptism, and God exacts the more from him to whom he has given the more; therefore since faith becomes dead by wicked works, why can it not be said that he suffers ship-wreck who falls from the grace of God into the hands of the devil? From which without Penance he cannot escape, or be renewed to such a condition that baptism may be profitable to him." Pages 300, 302.

"It troubles me exceedingly to hear how absurd, how impious, and how contradictory to themselves the trifles and babbles are, wherewith Luther bespatters the Sacrament of Penance." Page 318.

"Now let any one judge of the truth of Luther's opinion, who, contrary to the sentiments of all the Holy Fathers, draws the Keys of the Church to the laity, and to women, and says that these words of Christ, *Whatsoever you shall bind*, etc., are spoken not only to Priests, but also to all the faithful. Marcus Aemilius Scaurus, a man most excellent and of known honesty, being accused at Rome to the people by Varius Sucronensis, a man of little sincerity; his accuser having made a long and tedious discourse; Scaurus confidently relying on the judgment of the people, not thinking him worthy of an answer, said, 'Romans, Varius Sucronensis says it, Aemilius Scaurus denies it; which of them do you believe?' By which words the people, applauding this honorable man, scorned the idle accusations of the babbling adversary. Which discourse seems not more applicable to them, than to what we here state: for Luther says that the words of Christ concerning the Keys are spoken to the laity; St. Augustine denies it; which of them is the rather to be believed? Luther affirms, St. Ambrose denies; which of them has the greater credit? Finally, Luther affirms it, and the whole Church denies it; which do you think to be believed? But if anybody be so mad as to believe with Luther, that he ought to confess himself to a woman, perhaps it may not be amiss for him also to follow the other opinion of Luther, in which he persuades us not to be too careful in calling to mind our sins." Pages 336, 338.

"(Luther says), 'That God does nothing regard our works, nor has any need of them; but he has need that we should esteem him true in his promise.' What Luther meant by these words, he knows best himself. For my part, I believe that God cares for our faith and our works, and that He stands in need of neither our faith nor our works. For though God has no want of our goods, yet has He so much care of what we do that He commands some things to be done, and forbids other things: without whose care, not so much as one sparrow falls to the earth, five of which are sold for two farthings." Page 348.

"That Luther may understand that this Sacrament is no new thing, or vain fiction, but that it is so far from being void of grace that it confers the Spirit of grace and truth, we will here relate what St. Hierom has written of this *Sacrament of Confirmation*. 'If the bishop impose his hands, it is on them who have been baptized in the true faith, who have believed in the Father, Son, and Holy Ghost, three Persons and one substance. But the Arian, who believes in no other (stop your ears, that you may not be polluted with the words of such monstrous impiety), but in the Father alone, in Jesus Christ as a creature, in the Holy Ghost as servant to both; how shall he receive the Holy Ghost from the Church, who has not as yet obtained remission of his sins? For the Holy Ghost inhabits not, but where faith is pure, nor remains but in that Church which has true faith for her guide. If in this place you ask why he that is baptized in the Church receives not only the Holy Ghost but by the

The Lutheran Church

"Otherwise, if Luther persists in his distinction of the Pope's Church from Christ's, and in saying that the one has Orders for a Sacrament, the other not, let him show us the Church of Christ which, contrary to the faith of the Papal Church (as he calls it), knows not the Sacrament of Order. In the meanwhile it appears evidently that, by asserting this Sacrament to be unknown to the Church of Christ, and that they are not of Christ's Church who are governed by the Pope, he separates, by both these reasons, from Christ's Church, not only Rome, but also all Italy, Germany, Spain, France, Britain, and all other nations which obey the See of Rome, or have Orders for a Sacrament. Which people, being by him taken from the Church of Christ, it consequently follows that he must either confess Christ's Church to be in no place at all, or else, like the Donatists, he must reduce the Catholic Church to two or three heretics whispering in a corner." Pages 398, 400. "*All men do unanimously confess (Luther only excepted) that the Apostles were by our Savior ordained Priests at His Last Supper*, where it plainly appears that power was given them to consecrate the Body of Christ, which power the Priest alone hath. 'But,' says Luther, 'it is not a Sacrament, because there is no grace promised therein.' But pray, how or whence has he this knowledge? 'Because (says he) it is not read in the Scripture!' This is his usual consequence: 'Is it not written in the Gospels, therefore has it not been done by Christ.' Which form of reasoning the Evangelist overthrows when he says, *Many things were done*, *which are not written in this book."* Pages 404, 406.

"In this *Sacrament of Extreme Unction,* that Luther might be twice derided himself, he twice scoffs the Church: first, because Divines (says he) do call this Unction a Sacrament (as if those he calls Divines were the only men who call it a Sacrament). Again, because they call it Extreme; to which, as to the second, he himself objects, after a joking manner, what he can never answer in earnest: For it might be rightly called Extreme as being the last of four. Afterwards, to shew that it is no Sacrament, himself first objects, what he foresees everybody will object against him, viz. the words of St. James the Apostle, *'If any be sick amongst you, let him send for the Priests of the Church, and let them pray over him, anointing him with oil, in the name of our Lord: and the prayer of the faithful will save the sick, and our Lord will raise him up; and if he be in sins, they shall be forgiven him.'* These words (which, according to his own definition, most apparently testify Extreme Unction to be a Sacrament, as wanting neither a visible sign, nor promise of grace) he immediately begins, with most impudent confidence, to deride; as if they were of no manner of force. 'For my part (says he), I say, that if ever there was folly acted, it is especially in this place.' And I, again on the contrary do affirm, that if ever Luther was mad (as indeed his madness appears almost in every place), he is certainly distracted here, in the Sacrament of Extreme Unction, to an extreme height of madness." Pages 430, 432.

The Lutheran Church   133

"But though, as I said, I admire why Luther should be so much displeased at St. James's Epistle; yet, having read it more attentively, I wonder not at all; for, by the Apostle's writings, I find that he so narrowly touches Luther everywhere, as if, by his prophetic spirit, he had plainly foreseen him. For, when Luther under the pretext of faith, despises good works, St. James on the other side, disputes, by reason, Scripture, and example, *'that faith without works, is dead.'* Nor is it in one place alone, that by bitter words, he resists that prattling petulancy of Luther: *'If any one* (says he) *esteem himself religious, not bridling his tongue, but seducing his own heart, his religion is vain.'* Besides Luther frets at this, which he sees very fitly may be applied to his own tongue. *The tongue is a restless evil, full of deadly poison.* Finally he perceives that what the Apostle has writ against contentious persons is truly spoken against his own opinions. *'For* (says the Apostle) *who is wise and well disciplined among you? Let him show forth his works by a good conversation,* in the meekness of wisdom; *because if you have the zeal of souls, and contentions be in your hearts, do not glory, being liars against the truth. For this is not wisdom descending from above, from the Father of Lights, but an earthly, beastly, and diabolical wisdom: for where zeal is joined with contentions, there also is inconstancy, and every naughty work. But the wisdom which is from above, is first of all shamefaced, then peaceable, modest, compliable, agreeing with good things, full of mercy and good works, judging without dissimulation. And the fruit* of justice is sown in peace to the workers of peace.' These, gentle reader, are words which move Luther to wrath against the Apostle: these, I say, are the words whereby the Apostle as openly touches Luther's petulancy, railings, wicked and contentious objections; even as if he had seen him, and read his words. I question not but this Epistle, though never so much despised by Luther, will sufficiently prove to all Christians the Sacrament of Extreme Unction." Defence of the Seven Sacraments. Pages 446, 448, 450.

King Henry VIII. concludes his Defence of the Seven Sacraments with these memorable words: "But I beseech and entreat all other Christians, and through the bowels of Christ (whose faith we profess), to turn away their ears from the impious words and not to foster schisms and discords, especially at this time when most particularly it behooves Christians to be concordant against the enemies of Christ. Do not listen to the insults and detractions against the Vicar of Christ which the fury of the little monk spews up against the Pope; nor contaminate breasts sacred to Christ with impious heresies, for if one spews these he has no charity, swells with vain glory, loses his reason and burns with envy. Finally, with what feelings they would stand together against the Turks, against the Saracens, against anything infidel anywhere, with the same feelings they should stand together against this one little monk weak in strength." Page 462.

According to the latest statistics available there are 63,500,000 Lutherans in the world.

The Lutheran Church

QUESTIONS ON THE TEXT.

1. Who caused the schism between the Eastern and the Western Church?
2. Who was Photius?
3. Who was Caerelarius?
4. When did the Greek Orthodox Church come into existence?
5. In what does it mainly err?
6. What does Jesus say on disobedience to the Church He founded?
7. Upon whom did Jesus establish His Church?
8. Why are the members of the Greek Orthodox Church called schismatics?
9. Who was Martin Luther?
10. By what name are his followers generally known?
11. How many years after Christ did Luther found his Church?
12. What followed in the wake of the socalled Reformation?
13. Mention some of the doctrines which Luther denied.
14. By what Sacrament is the divine power given to consecrate?
15. What was Luther's teaching on the Blessed Sacrament?
16. What does Jesus teach on the subject?
17. In what words did Jesus confer the power to forgive sins?
18. Prove that Luther did not give the first German translation of the Bible to the world.
19. What does the learned Jesuit Coppens say anent Luther's study at the university at Erfurt?
20. Who wrote the Defence of the Seven Sacraments against Luther?
21. What title do the kings of England hold on account of the Defence of the Seven Sacraments?

The Episcopal Church

THE history of the Episcopal Church, also called Anglican Church, starts with the complicated love-story of an indecent, lustful, ruthless, and brutal king. Henry VIII. of England secretly married Anne Boleyn, whilst Catherine, his lawful wife, was still living. A few months later, Cranmer, Archbishop of Canterbury, Henry's servile creature, pronounced the king's first marriage null and void. In the same year, 1533, Pope Clement VII. annulled the decision of Cranmer and threatened the king with excommunication if he should fail within three months to restore Catherine of Aragon to her rights and dignity as queen. The three months passed. The king spurned the papal threat. The following year, March 23, the Holy Father declared the second marriage of Henry VIII. invalid. Thereupon Henry VIII. forced the Parliament, and Convocation in the spring of 1534, to make the king, instead of the Pope, the spiritual head of the Church of England. During the November session, 1534, his will was literally executed by the following enactment: "Be it enacted by the authority of this present Parliament that the king, our sovereign lord, his heirs and successors, kings of this realm, shall be taken, accepted and reputed the only supreme head on earth of the Church of England called Anglicana Ecclesia." A formal re-

The Episcopal Church

nunciation of fealty to the Pope followed the ensuing year. An immoral king caused the secession of England from the true Church.

The Church of England, as a separate church, dates back to the year 1534. A chasm of over fifteen hundred years yawns between the origin of the true Church and the scandalous establishment of the Episcopal Church. The Church, which Jesus founded, has existed about nineteen hundred years; but the Episcopal Church is scarcely four hundred years old. It is not the true Church, nor by any means a branch of the same. It has a purely human origin. History proves that the origin is only too human.

In the year 1554, through the influence of Cardinal Pole, England was reunited with Rome. The whole nation with very few exceptions rejoiced over this reunion with the Holy See. But the hope of religious peace was nipped in the bud.

In 1559 the Parliament upon the advice of the notorious Queen Elizabeth reimposed the oath of supremacy to be taken to the queen in all religious matters, abolished the sacrifice of Mass under penalties of confiscation and death. The bishops refused to accept such an imposition. Some 3,594 parishes were deprived of their pastors, because these pastors refused to take the oath of spiritual supremacy to the ungodly arrogant queen. Together with almost all the people, the Bishops and the Priests remained loyal to the Pope. They were deposed for it and imprisoned.

Thereupon Queen Elizabeth "through the plenitude of her ecclesiastical authority," appointed Matthew Parker as Archbishop of Canterbury. Parker was consecrated by the heretical ex-bishop Barlow, who probably was never validly consecrated himself, and who moreover used the corrupted Ordinal of Cranmer, without believing in the Church, in the Sacraments and in the Sacrifice of the Mass. From Parker all Anglican ordinations are derived. His ordination and that of all Anglican clergymen is simply invalid.

Though some Episcopalians love to appropriate the name of Catholic and have many doctrines and practices in common with the Catholic Church, it is in no way a branch of the same. It was a live-branch as long as it adhered to the tree of life. But it separated itself entirely from the tree, from the head and body of the Catholic Church.

From 1588 until the death of Queen Elizabeth, a period of fourteen years, Catholics were most cruelly persecuted, the best of them were consigned to the scaffold for no other reason than their fidelity to the Catholic Church. They were simply butchered. Their homes were confiscated. Priests were hunted down and when caught were tortured to death. Ordinary Catholic people lost their possession and citizenship for the reason that they attended Mass, or professed their loyalty to the Holy Father. "Some had their ears bored with a hot iron; others were publicly whipped." Lingard's History of England, Vol. 5: Page 515. For further information of the cruelties enacted against law-abiding Catholics during the reign of Elizabeth see Lingard's History of England, Vol. V., Pages 513-516.

The Church of England is divided into "High Church," "Low Church" and "Broad Church."

The "High Church" Anglicans regard the Church as a visible body organized under an equal confederated episcopal hierarchy. Therefore, they do not admit a supreme visible head. They believe in the seven Sacraments and in the power and authority of their bishops and lower clergy, whom they love to call priests. By their much-vaunted "branch theory," they attempt to prove the apostolic succession of their bishops through the Catholic Church, which they prefer to call the Roman Catholic branch.

Ever since the "Tractarian Movement," which began at Oxford in 1833 and flourished under Pusey and Newman, the High Church through the study of the Fathers has come back to many Catholic tenets and practices.

In consequence of this movement some returned to the Catholic Church; others copying most of our doctrines, practices and ritual services without admitting the primacy of the Pope and thus without entering the Catholic Church imitate it as closely as possible. They are known by the name of "Ritualists." Many of these ritualists lean towards union with the Holy See, and it is these that furnish most of the converts to the Church.

The "Low Church" looks on the Christian Church as an invisible society united by a purely spiritual bond; it denies the efficacy of the Sacraments.

The "Broad Church" Anglicans advocate most liberal toleration of conflicting doctrines and practices in the English Church.

Thanks to the grace of God and the deep studies which many of the Episcopal ministers are making of late, very many Episcopalians of all ranks have returned to the Catholic Faith. In October, 1909, a whole religious community of Episcopal Friars and Sisters at Graymoor, N. Y., came over in a body to the Catholic Church. Since that time another community of Sisters has followed their example.

These converts have one advantage: they know of the existence of seven Sacraments and many practices of the Church ere they enter; for the High Church Episcopals believe in seven Sacraments, recite prayers, attend vespers and conduct devotions very similar to those of the Catholic Church. The membership of the Episcopal Church is rated at 29,200,000.

The clergy of the High Church and of the Ritualistic Movement receive a good solid education. Many of them lead a life of voluntary celibacy. Let us hope that the better members of the Anglican establishment, who pray for the unity of the Church, may soon enter the true fold of Christ and find rest of soul. A prayer for the conversion of England is strictly in accord with the cordial wish of our Holy Father. Since of late years many members of the Anglican Church venerate the Blessed Virgin by the daily recital of the Rosary, we have reasons to hope that the ever-increasing influx from this denomination into the Catholic Church may continue: that many Episco-

The Episcopal Church

palians may find rest and security in the Catholic Church.

After a thorough inquiry into the claims of Anglican Orders, Pope Leo XIII., in 1896, came to the "settled and irrevocable" conclusion that they are "utterly null and void."

All Anglicans who sincerely wish a reunion of the Episcopal with the Catholic Church, must return unconditionally to the Church, from which their good ancestors were forced to separate themselves by a brutal king and then again by a wicked queen and an unscrupulous Parliament. With a maternal solicitude, the Catholic Church, as a good mother, awaits the return of her once fair daughter of England.

Presbyterian Church

AS a system of church government, Presbyterianism took shape in the "Institutes" of John Calvin. They assert that the government of the church belongs to the elders instead of to the bishops. The presbyteries, or associations of teaching and ruling elders, constitute the governing body. Without believing in the Sacrament of Holy Orders, these elders impose their hands upon the candidates and then call that ordination. Their highest court is the "General Assembly," composed of an equal number of ministers and ruling elders, delegated by the presbyters.

John Calvin is the accredited founder of the Presbyterian sect. John Knox (d. 1572), one of his disciples, a degraded apostate priest, who on account of his implication in the assassination of Cardinal Beaton, 1546, was chained to the galleys and served as prisoner for a year and a half. When released he began to preach Calvinistic doctrines and thus established Presbyterianism in Scotland. He agitated with might and main against the Catholic Church, against the holy sacrifice of the Mass, and all distinctly Catholic practices. In his fury against the Church, he roused the people by inflammatory harangues to a pitch of frenzy, encouraged them to enter the churches by violence, to break the images of the saints and even those of our

Lord, to sack the churches and set on fire the monasteries. This was done by the people of Perth. "The work of vandal destruction spread over a great part of the country. Among the historical edifices destroyed was the Carthusian monastery of Perth, the burial place of kings and queens, the magnificent cathedral at St. Andrew's, and the venerable abbey and palace of Scone, where the Scottish kings had been anointed and crowned for centuries. The lords of the Congregation received an important accession in the persons of Lord James Stuart, the half-brother of Mary Stuart, and the Earl of Argyle, who became the heads of the revolutionary movement. Burning and destroying on their way, the lords marched upon Edinburgh, sacked and demolished every religious edifice in the city, robbed the royal treasury and took possession of the mint." Guggenberger History of the Christian Era, Vol. 2, Page 216.

Now this John Knox, the instigator of vandalism, bloodshed and rebellion is the acknowledged champion of Presbyterianism. The open enemies of the Catholic Church honor him as one of the greatest reformers that ever lived. But history is a stubborn recounter of actual facts. "The evil that men do lives after them."

In his flattering history of Presbyterianism, William H. Lyon, the author of "A Study of the Sects," makes the following statements: "As a sect its most remarkable history and influence was in Scotland, where its champion was John Knox. It became to the country what Episcopalianism was in England— the rallying point of the nation against the ecclesiastical and political tyranny of Rome. In 1560 it became the Church of the kingdom; equally hostile to Catholicism, which it made punishable by death, and to Protestant dissenters."

The alleged ecclesiastical and political tyranny of Rome has its origin in the overheated brains of disgruntled, excommunicated public sinners and in the unbalanced minds of avowed bigots and persecutors of the Catholic Church.

Calvin's unfounded assertions are to a great extent the doctrines of the Presbyterian sects. He maintains that God had ordained the fall of man. As he says: "Cadit igitur homo, Dei providentia sic ordinante;" which means, "Man fell, because the Providence of God ordained it so." Institut., Lib. 3. Whereas Holy Scripture plainly indicates that Adam fell by the abuse of his freedom: he voluntarily ate of the forbidden fruit. Calvin, however, makes God the author of that sin. To impute a sin to God is blasphemy. Calvin gives the following explanation of predestination: "We call predestination that eternal decree of God, whereby He hath determined what the fate of every man should be. For not to the same destiny are all created: for, to some is allotted eternal life; to others eternal damnation. According as a man is made for one end or for the other, we call him predestined to life, or to death." Lib. 3, P. 337.

From this and many other passages of Calvin's own writings it is evident that he taught absolute predestination and reprobation. His teaching concerning predestination may be summarized in this sentence:

Presbyterian Church

Do what you please, God will send you to heaven or to hell, not in consequence of your work, but simply because of His immutable eternal decree. Predestination of this kind is one of the distinctive teachings of the Presbyterian denomination. In order to justify, as they think, their predestination theory, Presbyterians are wont to quote St. Paul. But St. Paul never even hints at a predestined eternal damnation. Their favorite text, taken from St. Paul's epistle to the Ephesians, is the following: "Blessed be the God and Father of our Lord Jesus Christ, who hath blessed us with spiritual blessings in heavenly places, in Christ: as he chose us in him before the foundation of the world, that we should be holy and unspotted in his sight in charity. Who hath predestined us unto the adoption of children through Jesus Christ unto himself: according to the purpose of his will: unto the praise of the glory of his grace, in which he hath graced us in his beloved son. In whom we have redemption through his blood, the remission of sins, according to the riches of his grace, which hath superabounded in us in all wisdom and prudence, that he might make known unto us the mystery of his will, according to his good pleasure, which he hath purposed in him, in the dispensation of the fullness of times, to re-establish all things in Christ, that are in heaven and on earth, in him. In whom we also are called by lot, being predestinated according to the purpose of him who worketh all things according to the counsel of his will. That we may be unto the praise of his glory, we who before hoped in Christ: In whom you also, after you had heard the word of truth (the gospel of your salvation); in whom also believing, you were signed with the holy Spirit of promise, who is the pledge of our inheritance, unto the redemption of acquisition, unto the praise of his glory." Eph. 1:3-14. In this whole passage St. Paul not even alludes to it that God had ever predestined anybody for hell. As a matter of fact, hell is a punishment for mortal sins: for bad acts wilfully committed. The wilful abuse of reason and free will deserves punishment.

In harmony with his unchristian theory of fatal predestination, Calvin holds that sanctifying grace is distinct and separate from the Sacrament of baptism, as a visible sign, and that this grace is only given to those who are predestined for heaven, and withheld from those whom Calvin by an imaginary eternal decree predestines for hell.

Besides baptism, Presbyterians also believe in the Lord's Supper. But in this as well as in the other Sacrament do they separate sanctifying grace from the actual reception of the Sacrament. They maintain that if a non-elect person receives the Lord's Supper, he receives but bread and wine; but if the justified receive the same species they receive Jesus Christ spiritually. Presbyterians do not believe in a bodily presence of Jesus Christ in the Blessed Eucharist.

Since no Presbyterian minister as such received valid ordination, or the Sacrament of Holy Orders, none of them has the power to consecrate, to change bread and wine into the body and blood of Jesus

Christ. Therefore, when Presbyterians receive what they call the Lord's Supper, they actually do not receive anything but bread and wine. They receive nothing spiritually except punishment for thus violently misinterpreting the plain words of Jesus Christ: "This is my body, which shall be delivered for you: this do for the commemoration of me. In like manner also the chalice, after he had supped, saying: This chalice is the new testament in my blood: this do ye, as often as you shall drink, for the commemoration of me." 1 Cor. 11:24, 25. "This is my body, which shall be delivered for you;" therefore, it is in all reality (and not in spirit only) the same body which was delivered for us on the cross, the day following.

Like the Lutheran denomination, Presbyterianism is divided into very many sects, each of them differing from the other. We hear of "Regular Presbyterians," "Old School Presbyterians," "New School Presbyterians," "Associated Presbyterians," "Reformed Presbyterians," "Northern Presbyterians," etc.

According to the latest statistics there are 8,633,000 Presbyterians in the world.

That the Presbyterian denominations cannot lay claim to a divine origin is conclusively proved by history. As a rule Presbyterians are laboring under many prejudices against the Catholic Church, though some of them are fair-minded and friendly toward the Catholics. Sincere converts from Presbyterianism to Catholicism are becoming more numerous from year to year. In the book "Distinguished Converts to Rome in America" (published 1907), we find twenty-four Presbyterians, among them six Presbyterian ministers and five sons and two daughters of ministers.

QUESTIONS ON THE TEXT.

1. Who is the founder of the Episcopal or Anglican Church?
2. Who was Henry VIII?
3. Who was Matthew Parker?
4. Mention the three main divisions of the Anglican Church.
5. What do you understand by the Tractarian Movement?
6. Who are the Ritualists?
7. Who is the founder of the Presbyterian Church?
8. Who was John Knox?
9. What was done by the people of Perth?
10. What is Calvin's teaching on Predestination?
11. What is St. Paul's teaching on Predestination?
12. What does St. Paul teach anent the Blessed Eucharist?
13. How many years after Christ was the Presbyterian Church founded?

Congregational Church

OWING to the influence of radical Protestantism, several of the ministers and members of the State Church of England were dissatisfied with the retention of so many Catholic rites, ceremonies, and practices, which they considered "popish tendencies." Thus innumerable factions arose with the avowed tendency of purifying the Anglican Church of all ceremonies and practices, which to them seemed unscriptural. These Puritans went so far as to decry as idolatry the wearing of a surplice, the use of the sign of the cross, kneeling at Communion, and invoking the saints.

In spite of fines, imprisonment, tortures, and several executions, these factions increased and were known as Independents. In 1580, at the age of thirty, *Robert Brown* wrote and circulated a number of pamphlets in which he assailed the State Church in unmitigating terms and propounded and advocated a new system of congregationally independent church government. He is regarded as the Father of modern Congregationalism. His stay in England being very unpleasant, Brown with some followers went to Holland. Several congregations were organized there, of which that at Leyden under the pastorate of John Robinson was the most flourishing. However, a stay in Holland seemed undesirable to many of the members, while a return to England appeared hopeless. In this predicament, over one hundred Puritans, or Independents, resolved to seek a peaceful home in the New World. Under the leadership of Elder William Brewster and Deacon Carver these "Pilgrim Fathers" set sail in the Mayflower, and in December, 1620, finally landed at Plymouth. The Puritans in America gradually adopted the name of Congregationalists.

Though history informs us that the slightest dissent with their preachers on Gospel truth was punished with scourging, exile, and even death, it is a peculiarity of Congregationalism that each congregation is entirely independent of any other Congregational community and that neither council, nor synod, nor any association of ministers has any right to prescribe to any particular congregation and that all pastors are of equal rank with regard to jurisdiction. No congregation can dictate to another. No council has the right to dictate, but only the privilege to advise. Every congregation enjoys autonomy. The spread of Congregationalism consists in a multiplication of independent parishes. The ministerial association, the ministers in general, have the right to sanction or to reject a minister; but they do not make the appointments. The congregation sends out a call to one or more ministers for a trial sermon. If he meets with the approval of the majority of the congregation he may be accepted. The natural danger in such a system is that the wealthier classes will bear undue influence on the teaching of the ministers. In their endeavor to eradicate local vices, chastise personal scandals, and warn against dangerous amusements, as well as in their doctrinal sermons, the ministers have to be very careful not to offend; otherwise their services will be no further required. In short, Congregationalists assume the right to do as they please and hire a minister for the purpose of influencing them to please to do what is right. Now if the minister succeeds in this, they are both doing well.

This assertion I make as a deduction of their parish autonomy, and by no means do I want to insinuate that the Congregationalists are in any way inferior in their morality or piety to other Protestant denominations.

Congregationalists believe in some spiritual apostolicity of the Church, an apostolicity, they say, which has nothing to do with personal succession. That apostolicity, they claim, was not always in the Church; but nevertheless it must have existed somewhere, for they claim to possess it now, even though they did not exist before the seventeenth century. Their apostolicity, like the fancies of a fairy tale, has only an imaginary existence.

Their theology at first was strictly Calvinistic, but during more recent times, they have drifted more and more towards rationalism of the Unitarian type. They differ from the Baptists in conceding to parents the right of having their children baptized in infancy.

In their self-government, they differ from all earlier denominations. However, they imagine that every Christian denomination is a part of the one true Church, though not as purely as their own. According to their theory, all Christians belong to the spiritual catholic church. In this sense they recite the words of the Apostles' Creed: "I believe in the one, holy catholic church, the communion of saints."

That there was no such parish autonomy in apostolic times is evident from the Acts of the Apostles. Since Congregationalists maintain that the Acts of the Apostles vouch for their theory of self-government, I deem it in place to cite a few quotations from those same Acts in order to show that they make a mistake in trying to prove the legitimacy of such independent government from that inspired source. "But Paul choosing Silas, departed, being delivered by the brethren to the grace of God. And he went through Syria and Cilicia, confirming the churches, *commanding them to keep the precepts of the apostles and the ancients.*" Acts 15:40, 41. "And as they (Paul and Timothy) passed through the cities, *they delivered unto them the decrees for to keep, that were decreed by the apostles and ancients who were at Jerusalem.*" Acts 16:4. Not the congregation, but the ancients of the church of Ephesus, received this instruction from St. Paul: "Take heed to yourselves, and to the whole flock, *wherein the Holy Ghost hath placed you bishops, to rule the church of God*, which he hath purchased with his own blood." Acts 20:28. "When the prince of pastors shall appear, you shall receive a never fading crown of glory." I. St. Peter 5:4.

There are 2,090,000 Congregationalists in the world.

Questions on the Text.

1. Who were the Puritans?
2. Who was Robert Brown?
3. Who were the Pilgrim Fathers?
4. When did they land in America?
5. Where did the Puritans adopt the name Congregationalists?
6. How many years before the Congregationalists came into existence did Jesus Christ found His Church?
7. How are Congregational ministers appointed?
8. Did St. Paul believe in such appointments?
9. Quote St. Paul on this subject.

Anabaptists

⋙ ⋘

THE Anabaptists—so called on account of their practice of rebaptizing those who had been baptized in infancy—followed in the wake of Lutheranism. *Nicholas Storch,* a cloth weaver and disciple of Luther, began to preach against infant baptism at Zwickau, Saxony. From among his adherents he chose twelve apostles and seventy disciples. In the year 1521 they were banished from Zwickau and came to Wittenberg. There Storch posed as a prophet, pretended to have visions and prophetic dreams, denounced all profane knowledge, rejected infant baptism, tried to impress his hearers with the alleged necessity of rebaptism and advocated his Free Republic of Christ, a commonwealth without either ecclesiastical or civil authority. Thomas Muenzer, and Andreas von Bodenstein, who is better known as Karlstadt, the name of his birthplace, Mark Thomas, Mark Stubner, Martin Cellarius, and a host of others assisted Storch in rousing the populace to such a pitch of fanaticism as to destroy altars, statues, and holy pictures in the churches.

"Undeniable as is the original affinity between the Anabaptists and the Lutherans, yet this affinity soon changed into a mutual opposition, the most decided. An indescribable confusion prevailed in the minds of the new sectaries, and a fearful fanaticism drove them

Anabaptists

on to every species of extravagance and violence; and as they had the inmost conviction of doing all things by the impulse of the Divine Spirit, all hope of opposing their errors by rational instruction was utterly fruitless. Muenzer was deeply implicated in the war of the peasants." J. A. Moehler, Symbolism, Article 55.

In the year 1522 Luther left the Wartburg and hastened to Wittenberg to denounce and oust the fanatic leaders, Storch, Muenzer, and Karlstadt, from that city. He succeeded in banishing them.

Thomas Muenzer started a commonwealth in Muehlhausen, led his people to war and was defeated. He was executed in the year 1525, having been reconciled with the Church.

Storch died at Munich in 1525; Karlstadt at Basel in the year 1541.

Louis Hetzer, another Anabaptist leader, took twelve wives and openly defended adultery as pleasing to God. He was beheaded at Constance 1529.

In 1534, the Anabaptists assumed the dictatorship at Muenster in Westphalia. People were rebaptized in crowds. Those who refused to submit to a second baptism were abused and banished from their own city. They joined their Prince-Bishop who led an army against the usurpers at Muenster. John Bockelson was one of their principal instigators. John von Leyden proudly conducted himself as the tyrant-king of the New Sion (Muenster). He had seventeen wives. His fanaticism rose with his much vaunted success until his utter defeat in 1535. John von Leyden was executed together with his chancellor Krechting and the "royal executioner" Knipperdolling. Their bodies were placed in an iron cage and suspended from the steeple of St. Lambertus church. This put an end to Anabaptism at Muenster. After this the Anabaptists were persecuted everywhere; and for a number of years their history was written in the blood of their members.

These Anabaptists had announced a free republic of Christ, a perfect life, in which neither rulers nor laws, not even the Bible would be needed, but wherein the moral law written in man's heart would be the guiding norm of life. They dreamt of perfect equality among men, of free love, and the abolition of all hostilities and wars at the very time when human blood flowed so copiously on the battle-fields. These Anabaptists believed themselves destined to prepare the way for the approach of their imaginary millennium. They did not baptize their children, but allowed them to grow up in the state of original sin exposed to the danger of dying deprived of sanctifying grace. Jesus said to Nicodemus: "Unless a man be born again of water and the Holy Ghost, he cannot enter into the kingdom of God." St. John 3:5.

For an Anabaptist both Baptism and the Holy Eucharist have only a figurative signification. When Jesus Christ tells us of the absolute necessity of Baptism in order to enter the kingdom of God, they foist their foolish opinion of a figurative signification upon their members. When Jesus Christ plainly says with reference to the Blessed Eucharist: *This is my Body;*

Anabaptists

This is my Blood; they maintain that it is only a figure and a sign of mutual love, the same as any ordinary banquet or luncheon.

"With peculiar bitterness did these sectarians declare themselves against the Lutheran doctrine of Justification, and in this respect, they almost come round to the Catholic point of view." J. A. Moehler, Symbolism, Art. 57. Some of them admitted original sin, others denied it in order to assail infant baptism. Some Anabaptists denied the divinity of Christ; others, that He received His human nature from the Blessed Virgin Mary. Some asserted that finally all would convert, not even excluding the devil himself; others maintained that the souls of the departed are in a state of sleep until judgment day. These, however, were the opinions which some Anabaptists tried to force upon the faithful; but as the learned Moehler remarks in his "Symbolism," they "should not be considered as strictly Anabaptist; for, in part they were in direct opposition to other maxims of the sect. It is, on the contrary, to be presumed that at the commencement, amid the general religious ferment of the age, a multitude of men joined the Anabaptists without having anything akin to them, save a dark fanaticism and confusion of ideas. But in general the remark holds good that the first Anabaptists had neither a compact system of theology, nor any body of doctrines however ill-connected, which all uniformly professed. If we consider that their sect had not originated in one man as the common center of all; and that the leading idea, round which all revolved, though powerful enough to inspire enthusiasm, was yet, in a doctrinal point of view, unproductive; if we consider, moreover, that the dark feelings by which all were animated and impelled had not received a definite expression in any public formulary—a circumstance which gave occasion to a general complaint on the part of their adversaries—we shall feel the less surprised at the fact above mentioned." J. A. Moehler, Symbolism, Article 58. Moreover, the Anabaptists maintained that anyone who felt himself moved, as he thought, by the Spirit, should prophesy and preach.

Mennonite Church

MENNO SIMONIS, formerly pastor of the Catholic congregation in Withmarsum, Holland, became prominent as an Anabaptist organizer in 1536. He disavowed any sympathy for and connection with the fanatic Anabaptists of Muenster. But he rejected infant baptism. He strove to moderate the social upheaval of the sect, urged them on to lead a quiet life, forbade them to take an oath and to carry weapons, and emphasized strict obedience to authority. He found a great following. In the year 1561 he died to the great regret of his followers, who are called Mennonites unto this day. Even during his life-time, his adherents divided into two factions, the "Fine" and the "Coarse" Anabaptists, or Mennonites. The "Fine" faction claims to adhere closer to the authority of the older Anabaptists, whereas the "Coarse" more closely resemble other Protestant sects.

As we find them in this country, the Mennonites generally are good, honest, obedient citizens, somewhat secluded, industrious and modest both in dress and demeanor. Converts from the Mennonites make good loyal Catholics. Though all authors of repute maintain that Mennonites and Anabaptists are interchangeable terms, the Mennonites themselves call in question their descent from the earlier Anabaptists.

While the Mennonites admit that the sinfulness of Adam was inherited by all his children, they do not believe in the transmission to posterity of the sin itself. They claim that the guilt of sin was not incurred by his progeny. This inherited sinfulness inclines man to sin. They do not deny the free will of man. Schyn, in his History of the Mennonites (Historiae Mennonitarum plenior Deductio, Article V, P. 176) tells us: "Eidem jam lapso et perverso inerat facultas occurrens et a Deo oblatum bonum audiendi, admittendi, aut rejiciendi," i.e., "Even after his fall and perversion man had the faculty to listen to, approve of, or reject the good that presents itself and is proffered by God."

They maintain that on account of the effused Blood of Jesus Christ, we, by living faith which worketh charity, acquire true justice, the condoning or the forgiveness of all past and present sins. They do not believe in the Sacrament of Penance and overlook the fact that Jesus Christ gave the power to forgive and the power to retain sins to His Apostles and their rightful successors, and that the condition for the forgiveness has been placed by God and must not be placed but be fulfilled by the sinner. "He breathed on them; and He said to them: Receive ye the Holy Ghost. Whose sins you shall forgive, they are forgiven them; and whose sins you shall retain, they are retained." St. John 20:22, 23. Contrary to the earlier Anabaptists, the Mennonites declare against polygamy. Their ministers are elected and then confirmed by the imposition of the hands on the part of the elders. The washing of feet of the traveling brethren is one of their ceremonies. Impenitent sinners among them are exhorted, and if they do not improve upon this exhortation they are excommunicated, and then must be shunned even socially.

The aggregate membership of the Mennonites is 87,164.

They have split up into as many as seventeen different bodies.

Baptist Church

THOUGH the members of this denomination delight in boasting of their origin as that of the primitive Church and refuse to acknowledge any name of a human founder of their sect, it is nevertheless an historical fact, that their origin dates back to the beginning of the seventeenth century, and moreover, that their sect was not founded in Palestine but in England.

Dr. Armitage, a Baptist, in his book, "A History of the Baptists," made a vain attempt to trace the Baptists, even before they existed, by their vital principles and practices from the time of our Lord and Savior Jesus Christ until the year 1886. It is generally known, not only among philosophers but among all people blessed with common sense, that *a thing cannot act before it exists*. The Baptists certainly had no practices before they were in existence. Their practices at most may be similar to those of others who lived before them; but their own principles and practices do not antedate their origin, which, as history tells us, was in the seventeenth century. For the love of truth Baptists ought to admit the historical fact of their very recent origin, and should not attempt to foist their pet theory of an imaginary apostolicity upon the world. People have a right to know the truth.

W. H. Lyon in "A Study of the Sects," P. 119, says: "It was in Holland that the English Independents, or Brownists, first came into contact with Anabaptist doctrines; and one of their ministers in Amsterdam, the Rev. John Smyth, became a convert to them, and formed a new church, part of which came to London in 1612. The early history of the sect *there* is uncertain; but it is known that the church existed in 1633, and from that time adherents multiplied fast." The most reliable information we get from Hergenroether in his excellent Kirchengeschichte, Vol. 3, P. 533. He writes: "The Baptists originated in England about the year 1608, independent of the Mennonites of Germany and Holland. They obtained some prominence after the year 1688. They administered Baptism (to adults only) by immersion and tenaciously adhered to the Calvinistic doctrines of predestination and justification, celebrated the Sabbath instead of the Sunday and entertained antinomian views."

In common with other denominations, they maintain that the Bible is the only rule of faith and religious practice, and that, moreover, everybody may interpret Holy Scripture according to his own private notions without any guidance save his own human knowledge. This is their doctrine in theory; in practice every parishioner is expected to adopt the views of the preacher. Private interpretation of the Bible after all amounts to this: read and interpret the Bible as you please, but be sure to agree with the notion of your minister and the general view of the congregation, for by them you will be condemned, if you don't.

Baptists hold that baptism, in order to be valid, must be by immersion and can be validly administered by those only who profess personal faith in Jesus Christ, and can be validly received by those only who have an intelligent faith. They reject infant baptism.

As to their mode of baptism, namely by immersion, it is the one that was generally practiced in the early days of the Church. If all other conditions requisite for baptism are complied with, then immersion is valid baptism. Immersion, however, was not the only mode of baptism used in the earlier days of the Church.

Upon the sermon of St. Peter at Jerusalem on Pentecost day about three thousand were converted and were baptized the same day. Now, it seems hardly possible that these three thousand were baptized by immersion, even if all the disciples kept on immersing the converts till midnight. The general opinion is that these three thousand were not baptized by immersion. So much is certain, there is no passage in Holy Scripture from which we might infer that they were led to the flowing water and then immersed. "They, therefore, that received his word were baptized; and there were added in that day about three thousand souls." Acts 2:41. Take the case of the eunuch, whom St. Philip converted and baptized in the river; even there we have no reason to suppose upon the authority of the Bible only, that baptism was by immersion; it may have been by pouring the

Baptist Church

water on the convert. "They went down into the water, both Philip and the eunuch: and he baptized him. And when they were come up out of the water, the Spirit of the Lord took away Philip; and the eunuch saw him no more. And he went on his way rejoicing." Acts 8:38, 39.

When a person goes down into the water of a river it simply means that he descends from the bank of the river into the water. It does not imply that the person gets under the water with his whole body, head and all. Neither does the Scripture suggest such a ducking here. For both went into the water. If both were entirely under the water how could Philip baptize? If Philip was not under the water, but simply in the water, then the eunuch was not under it either, for the Bible says: "They went down into the water, both Philip and the eunuch." When a person gets out of a river, he comes up out of the water. Holy Scripture does not suggest any immersion in the baptism of the eunuch. How he was baptized is a matter of conjecture; the Bible does not tell us. With those who want no tradition in religious matters, but claim to take the Bible for the sole rule, the cases so far mentioned cannot be adduced as proof of their immersion theory. The expression of St. Peter (Acts 10:47) seems to exclude the idea of baptism by immersion. "Then Peter answered: Can any man forbid water, that these should not be baptized, who have received the Holy Ghost, as well as we?" Now to *forbid water* rather implies to prohibit taking or receiving water. In this instance it means the receiving of baptismal water, the water of baptism, without indicating the mode of procedure.

Baptists refer to the Letter of St. Paul to the Romans, Chap. 6, V. 4, as a proof of their assumption that immersion can be proved from the Bible. Let us read that text and see whether it proves anything in favor of their mode of baptism: "For we are buried together with him by baptism into death; that as Christ is risen from the dead by the glory of the Father, so we also may walk in newness of life." Rom. 6:4. I candidly admit that with the aid of tradition we can prove baptism by immersion from this passage; but without this assistance, the words do not prove it; for St. Paul does in no way speak here of the mode of baptism, but merely institutes a comparison to urge the faithful to walk in the footsteps of Christ. Buried by baptism, if buried means simply covered, might mean to be soaked by rain, to be saturated by pouring or sprinkling. If buried by baptism is spoken in a figurative sense, then it will not do to draw a literal meaning from it.

Upon the authority of the Fathers, I believe that the passage in question refers to baptism by immersion. But Baptists acknowledge no such authority.

They use another passage of Scripture in proof of their teaching with regard to baptism by immersion. It is taken from the Letter of St. Paul to the Colossians, Chap. 2, V. 12: "*Buried* with him in baptism, in whom also you are risen again by the faith of the operation of God, who hath raised him up from the dead." Buried with him in baptism, if taken literally, would imply, that *actually put under water* we were with Christ, or together with Him covered with water. The meaning of the expression "buried with him in baptism" the Bible nowhere explains. People who do not acknowledge tradition should be slow to venture an opinion on this text.

I might bring a similar text with a figurative meaning, and assert that sprinkling of the heart and washing of the body was the original mode of baptism. St. Paul furnishes the text. "Let us draw near with a true heart in fulness of faith, having our *hearts sprinkled* from an evil conscience, and our *bodies washed* with clean water." Heb. 10:22.

But what would you think of me, if I asserted, contrary to all denominations, that baptism must be in a mode similar to the floating of the ark of Noe? St. Peter writes: "He preached to those spirits that were in prison: which had been some time incredulous, when they waited for the patience of God in the days of Noe, when the ark was a building: wherein a few, that is, eight souls, were saved by water. Whereunto *baptism being of the like form*, now saveth you also." I. Peter 3:19-21. However, I do not maintain such folly; for I am aware of the fact that figurative speech must be taken in a figurative sense, which in this instance conveys the following idea: as the ark was the means by which the eight persons in it escaped the deluge, so baptism is a means of your salvation, a means of escaping eternal damnation.

Anybody who tries to prove from the Bible that

immersion is the only valid mode of baptism, attempts the impossible. The Bible does not vouch for such an assumption. On the contrary, the Bible, as I have proved, suggests the idea that baptism was not always administered by immersing the person. The Catholic Church maintains that baptism by immersion, by pouring, and by aspersion or sprinkling, may be valid; that whenever the form and matter of baptism, i. e., the words and the water, are administered at the same time with the intention to baptize an unbaptized human being, a valid baptism takes place. For various reasons, however, the Church prescribes baptism by pouring. Except in cases of necessity, the other modes are at present illicit at least in the Latin Church; but they are valid nevertheless.

Baptists reject infant baptism as unscriptural. But their *rejection* of infant baptism is rather unscriptural, nay even anti-scriptural. The Bible nowhere forbids infant baptism. The forbidding of infant baptism is, therefore, unscriptural. The Bible tells us that, "unless a man be born again of water and the Holy Ghost, he cannot enter into the kingdom of God" (St. John 3:5); and that the little ones are destined for the kingdom of God: "for the kingdom of heaven is for such" (St. Matt. 19:14); if they are destined for it and cannot enter it without being born of water and the Holy Ghost, i. e., without baptism, then children must be baptized. The rejection of infant baptism is, therefore, anti-scriptural. That children of converts to Christianity were baptized is suggested in the Bible. Of the keeper of the prison it is said: "He himself was baptized, and all his house immediately." Acts 16:33. To *all his house* probably some little ones belonged. "And I baptized also the household of Stephanus." I. Cor. 1:16. "And Crispus, the ruler of the synagogue, believed in the Lord, with all his house; and many of the Corinthians hearing, believed, and were baptized." Acts 18:8.

Baptists regard baptism as a mere symbol, as a sign, but not as a means of canceling sins, "But Peter said to them: *Do penance, and be baptized every one of you in the name of Jesus Christ, for the remission of your sins:* and you shall receive the gift of the Holy Ghost." Acts 2:38. "And now why tarriest thou? Rise up, and be baptized, and wash away thy sins, invoking his name." Acts 22:16. "For you are all the children of God by faith, in Christ Jesus. For as many of you as have been baptized in Christ, have put on Christ." Gal. 3:26, 27. Baptism, therefore, according to Holy Scripture is a means of washing away sins, the putting on of Christ which implies conferring sanctifying grace and a right to the kingdom of heaven. It is not a *mere symbol*. It is more than that: it is an absolutely necessary means of salvation; but it may be received either actually, or by baptism of blood (martyrdom) or by desire.

With reference to the Blessed Eucharist, the Baptists believe in a merely symbolical meaning of the Last Supper. St. Paul held a different view: "Take ye, and eat; this is my body, which shall be delivered

170   *Christian Denominations*

for you." I. Cor. 11:24. The body of Christ that was delivered for us on Calvary was not a mere symbol, but an actual body. The same actual Body He gave to His disciples, saying: "Take ye and eat." The symbol theory is unscriptural. Such is the irony of fate, or better, the anomaly of facts, that heretics claim to be scriptural in the very things where Holy Scripture is plainly against them. The true Body and Blood of Jesus Christ were given by Him to His Apostles. True Christians still receive the same Body and Blood of Jesus substantially in Holy Communion.

As might be logically expected, private interpreters of the Bible will have divergent private views, and those wanting all requisite knowledge to read and interpret the Bible intelligently will come to some foolish conclusions. So it happened. The Baptists, as well as other private interpreters of the Holy Bible, began to quarrel among themselves on some doctrinal points or on some religious practices and disintegrated into various sects. *Roger Williams*, who organized the first Baptist congregation in America, in Rhode Island, 1639, soon saw where private interpretation leads to.

Some of the better known Baptist denominations in America are mentioned here.

The General Baptists are those Baptists who believe, as we Catholics do, that Jesus Christ died for all mankind. "But all things are of God, who hath reconciled us to himself by Christ; and hath given *to us the ministry of reconciliation*. For God indeed was in Christ, reconciling the *world* to himself, not imputing to them their sins; and he hath placed in us the word of reconciliation." II. Cor. 5:18, 19. Speaking of the sin of Adam and the redemption *through Christ*, St. Paul says: "Therefore, as by the offence of one, unto *all men* to condemnation; so also by the justice of one, unto *all men* to justification of life." Rom. 5:18.

The Particular Baptists maintain that Christ died for the elect only, and that they themselves belong to these elect, the chosen few.

The Seventh-Day Baptists, who formerly went by the name of "Sabbatarian Baptists" in England, observe the seventh day instead of the Sunday. This is in perfect harmony with their rule of faith, Scripture only.

The Six Principle Baptists have six principles, or doctrines: Repentance, Faith, Imposition, Baptism, Resurrection, and the Eternal Judgment.

The Dunkards, or "German Baptists," also called "Brethren," were founded in Germany by Alexander Mack about 1708. They baptize adults only by threefold immersion and seek to be excessively simple in language, habits, dress and demeanor.

The Free Baptists came into existence in New Hampshire in 1780 through the efforts of Benjamin Randall. Being dissatisfied with Congregationalism there, he went to Berwick, Me., where he joined the Baptists. But he did not believe in unconditional predestination as the rest of the Baptists in Berwick did, who were strictly Calvinistic. In his sermons he frequently spoke of a general atonement and the sinner's ability to accept Christ. For this reason he was disfellowshipped. Then he organized the first Free Baptist congregation at Durham, N. H., without really intending to start a new sect. In 1851 the ceremony of feet-washing, which until then had been obligatory, became optional. In consequence of which some Free Baptists have done away with it. They do not insist on baptism in their own denomination as a requisite to partake of the Communion of the Lord's Table, but practice an "open communion."

We must bear in mind that their so-called communion is nothing more than eating and drinking together in memory of our Lord's Passion and Death. For such common eating and drinking baptism is certainly not necessary. But for the reception of what Catholics understand by Holy Communion; namely the partaking of the Body and Blood of Jesus Christ, baptism is necessary; for Holy Communion must be received in the state of sanctifying grace and by a Christian only, but baptism is the only door to Christianity. No unbaptized person is a Christian.

The Primitive Baptists, also called *Old School, Anti-Mission and Hard Shell Baptists* date back to the year 1835. They are opposed to missions, Sunday schools, and to all religious institutions. Their religion is extremely gloomy, being that of rigid Calvinism: *total depravity* of human nature, and unconditional election and reprobation.

The Separate Baptists of today have this in common with the Free Baptists that they do not hold the harsh and absolutely false theory of Calvinistic predestination and reprobation. They believe in God's justice, but like all Baptists reject infant baptism and nearly all the Sacraments.

The United Baptists arose about the middle of the 18th century when a futile attempt was made to unite the Regular and the Separate Baptists. The result was an additional denomination. Feet-washing is one of their important ceremonies.

The Old-Two-Seed-In-The Spirit Predestinarian Baptists, like the Manicheans of old, believe in two eternal principles, one good, the other evil, which they call the seed of life and the seed of death. They originated during the first half of the nineteenth century, eighteen hundred years too late to claim a Christian origin.

The Winebrennerians, the followers of John Winebrenner, who adopted the pretentious designation of *"Church of God,"* date back to the year 1830. Their three ordinances as mere symbols are Baptism, Feet-washing, and the Lord's Supper. Their church government is congregational.

The Campbellites, also known as *Disciples of Christ,* or *Christians,* came into existence about the year 1817. Thomas Campbell and his son Alexander were their first leaders. They claim to believe in the Bible without any creed. Though they maintain not to hold any creed, their creed is that the Bible is the unerring and all sufficient word of God. A belief in the Bible without a creed is an impossibility. He who considers the Bible the unerring word of God has at least that creed. Campbellites care little for logic and principle. Their literature is poor and consists largely of ranting (without proving anything) against other Christian denominations, especially Catholics.

Admitted that the Holy Bible is God's unerring word, it by no means follows that every reader or even any reader of the Bible is exempt from error. A person who has not the requisite knowledge cannot read the Holy Bible intelligently, much less unerringly. The generality of mankind does not acquire this knowledge. Does not the history of Protestantism prove sufficiently that private interpretation and the arrogant claim of individual infallibility in reading and explaining the Bible has led to the most contradictory creeds? The reader of the unerring word of God is very liable to err. Such is the lesson of history. People who altogether reject Tradition can never get at the true meaning of many biblical passages.

"Thou wilt obtain the knowledge full and entire of the Christian religion only in connection with its essential form, which is the Church. Look at the Scripture in an ecclesiastical spirit, and it will present thee an image perfectly resembling the Church. Contemplate Christ in, and with His creation—the Church—the only adequate authority—the only authority representing Him, and thou wilt then stamp His image on thy soul. Should it, however, be stated, in ridicule of this principle, that it were the same as to say: 'Look at the Bible through the spectacles of the Church;' be not disturbed, for it is better for thee to contemplate the star by the aid of a glass, than

Baptist Church

to let it escape thy dull organ of vision, and be lost in mist and darkness. Spectacles, besides, thou must always use, but only beware lest thou get them constructed by the first casual glass-grinder, and fixed upon thy nose." Dr. J. A. Moehler, Symbolism, Article 39.

Baptists of all descriptions throughout the whole world number about 9,230,000.

Questions on the Text.

1. In what century did the Anabaptist create havoc in human society?
2. Who were their notorious leaders?
3. What did Jesus say to Nicodemus concerning the necessity of Baptism?
4. Who is the founder of the Mennonite Church?
5. What is their error on original sin?
6. Which doctrine of Christ do they ignore relative to forgiving of sins?
7. When and where did the Baptist Church originate?
8. What is their mode of baptizing?
9. Why is the rejection of infant baptism unscriptual and even antiscriptual?
10. What does St. Peter say about Baptism?
11. What does St. Paul write to the Galatians anent Baptism?
12. What do you understand by the Baptist symbol theory?
13. Prove its fallacy.
14. What is Holy Communion?
15. What is the result of private interpretation of the Bible?

Moravians

BOHEMIAN BRETHREN

MORAVIANS, or Bohemian Brethren, date back to the first part of the eighteenth century. There was a society with the same name previous to this, but it lasted only 94 years. It was organized in 1457 in Moravia and governed by twenty-eight elders according to mutually adopted principles of doctrine. Their usual name was "Brethren and Sisters of the Law of Christ" or simply "Brethren." At their synod at Lhotka, they agreed to separate entirely from the Catholic Church. Three of their men were consecrated bishops by the Waldensian bishop Stephen. They soon disbanded partly on account of internal troubles but mainly on account of persecution. Most of them joined Protestant denominations. The society was almost totally dismembered.

In 1722 Nicholas Louis Count Zinzendorf, a Lutheran, organized a religious community on his estate Berthelsdorf, Saxony, under the pastorate of Andrew Rothe. Among the members were people from Moravia. After five years the new religious colony numbered about 300. Disregarding dogmatic differences Count Zinzendorf urged them on to what he considered practical piety. The colony increased.

A new congregation was organized on the Hutberg, which received the name of Herrnhut. From this name the appellation Herrnhuters is derived, a name by which these people are called in Germany. Factions arose. Most of the members were dissatisfied with Andrew Rothe. In order to unite the quarrelling factions, Count Zinzendorf became bishop, and twelve elders were elected by the people. All went by the name of "Brethren." Later on Count Zinzendorf assumed the title "Ordinary of the Brethren." He died in 1760.

These Brethren, or Moravians, as they are more frequently called, have set formulas universally used for infant baptism and for the baptism of adults. Before they receive the Last Supper, they hold a love-feast, make a general confession of sinfulness and receive some admonitions and practical instructions from their minister. Communion, or, as they prefer to call it, the Sacrament of the Lord's Supper, is received kneeling. Moreover, they have conformity in their rites of confirmation, ordination, and the burial of the dead. Formerly, they frequently resorted to casting lots in order to divine the will of God. The selection of young couples for marriage was likewise by lot. Feet-washing is one of their liturgical services. The highest legislative authority among the Bohemian Brethren is vested in the General Synod held once every ten years.

In virtue of "the cross and blood theology" the Moravians, or United Brethren, frequently meditate (and their ministers, as a rule, often preach) on the sufferings and the bloody death of Jesus on the cross, which praiseworthy practice has a good moral influence on their daily life. Undoubtedly, when members of this sect get the grace of conversion to the Catholic Church, they are well prepared to appreciate the devotion of the Way of the Cross and the grand ceremonies of Holy Week.

In the United States the little society of Bohemian Brethren or Moravians numbers 37,242.

Friends, or Quakers

GEORGE FOX, born in Leicestershire, 1624, a shoemaker by trade, is the founder of this Christian denomination. He began to preach his new religion in 1647, and died January 13, 1691. His followers call themselves the Society of Friends; by outsiders they are more generally styled Quakers, which term, though originally a nickname, is no longer considered such.

Their central dogma, towards which everything in their teaching and practice converges, is the doctrine concerning the "Inner Light," a sort of individual inspiration of the Holy Ghost. Sacraments, creeds, and councils are adjudged superfluous external practices. Human learning, though valued, is not considered necessary in their ministry. Their meetings, as a rule, commence in silence. Everybody is supposed to pray to the Holy Ghost for light. If anyone, man, woman or child in the congregation believes himself or herself moved by this "Inner Light," this person gets up and speaks "by the Holy Ghost." As a rule, their ministers do not receive a stipulated salary, but are supposed to do their work for the love of truth or instruction. The members of the Society may give liberally towards the support of the minister, who is permitted to accept whatever is offered him as long as he does not use his ministry for the precise purpose of making money. Generally speaking, they have no regularly ordained ministers.

The liturgy of the Friends is as simple as you can imagine it. They believe that all symbolic rites were abolished by our Savior on the cross and that He announced this in the words: "It is finished," "It is consummated." Actually, Jesus indicated by these words that His passion was consummated, that His death was at hand, and that through His passion and death redemption was completed. Jesus never referred to the abolition of Christian symbolic rites at any time in His life; in fact He instituted them.

The word "Trinity" is in disfavor with them, since they cannot find it in the Bible; but, nevertheless, they believe in the Blessed Trinity, or, as they would say, in the Godhead of the Father, and of the Son, and of the Holy Ghost, which, however, really means the same. The Friends are truly advocates of peace. They were foremost in advocating the abolition of slavery, not by war, but in a peaceable way. Wars are looked upon as abominations, which they undoubtedly are. Balls are branded as "nurseries of debauchery and wickedness." But in spite of this prohibition it sometimes happens, as is the case with members of all denominations that young couples transgress the precept of well-meaning ministers, perhaps more on account of youthful levity than from any evil intent. Sacred concerts, oratorios, and operatic singing, the Friends do not permit. They try to foster interior devotion to the best of their knowledge, and avoid cursing and swearing. In their dress and mode of

Friends, or Quakers

living they are very simple and modest and well worthy of imitation in these days of fashion and high living.

Owing to doctrinal disputes, the Friends soon began to split into dissenting sects such as *Orthodox* and *Hicksite*, *Wilburite* and *Primitive* Quakers. In America they number about 119,600.

Converts from the Society of Friends to the Catholic Church appreciate the wealth of spiritual aid, the well nigh unlimited opportunities of laying up treasures for heaven, which the Catholic Church, wherein Jesus dwells, offers them.

Methodist Church

JOHN WESLEY, born in 1703, as the son of an Anglican minister, is recognized as the founder of Methodism. Without at first intending to leave the Established Church, he established another, which he intended as a revival within the churches. With his brother Charles, his friend George Whitefield, and several other students at Oxford, he held small evening meetings for spiritual meditations. John was the organizer, his brother Charles the poet, and George Whitefield the orator of the movement. In their studies as well as in their meetings, they proceeded methodically. For this reason they were soon nicknamed Methodists. In the year 1728, John Wesley was ordained as minister of the Anglican Church; though he never obtained charge of a parish nor ever gained the friendship of other Anglican clergymen. From the Moravians (Herrnhuters), he copied his pietistic views of conversion, Spirit assurance and other eccentricities.

On the 1st of May, 1738, some forty or fifty of his followers agreed to meet with him every Wednesday evening and to spend some time in prayer, spiritual conversation and singing. These meetings were opened and closed with prayer. Methodists date their denomination back to May, 1738. It is said that on May 24, 1738, John Wesley experienced that desirable sudden change within himself, which he henceforth endeavored to produce in others. For a time some of his ministers preached in the open air. But as early as May, 1739, the cornerstone of the first Methodist meeting-house was laid in London.

The Wesleys drew up a set of articles of doctrine (twenty-five in number) which were intended to serve as a broad basis on which all Christians might unite; which pious wish, needless to say, was never realized. Anyone who was anxious "to flee the wrath of God, to come and to be saved from sin" was deemed fit for membership. The sins of cursing, Sabbath-breaking, intoxication, cheating, fighting, vanity in dress and other prevalent evils were strictly forbidden. On the other hand, the corporal works of mercy John Wesley highly recommended to all his followers. Besides, he inspired his listeners with religious enthusiasm. Though he himself professed his belief in the seven Sacraments, his followers, Methodists in general, admit only two: Baptism and the Lord's Supper.

Even during the lifetime of the above mentioned founders, there was a schism in their own ranks. The followers of Whitefield sternly clung to the cheerless and gloomy doctrine of Calvinistic predestination, while this was rejected by the Wesleyan Methodists.

Infant baptism is commanded, because infants belong to the Kingdom of God. For a Methodist, however, baptism is merely a sign of the regeneration which the recipient obtains previously to the reception of baptism. In this as in many other things Methodism differs from the Catholic Church, which teaches that baptism bestows sanctifying grace, makes the recipient a child of God, and an heir of heaven. Jesus said to Nicodemus: "Unless a man be born again of water and the Holy Ghost, he *cannot enter* into the kingdom of God." St. John 3:5. Without baptism, the being born of water and the Holy Ghost, no man can enter the kingdom of God. Now Jesus wants the little ones to belong to this kingdom; for He said: "Suffer the little children, and forbid them not to come to me: for the kingdom of heaven is for such." St. Matt. 19:14. They must be baptized in order to enter the kingdom of God. Original sin must be effaced. "But Peter said to them: Do penance, and be baptized every one of you in the name of Jesus Christ, for the remission of your sins." Acts 2:38. Baptism, therefore, remits sin. "Rise up, and be baptized, and wash away thy sins, invoking his name." Acts 22:16. St. Paul writes: "Not by the works of justice, which we have done, but according to his mercy, he saved us, by the laver of regeneration (baptism), and renovation of the Holy Ghost; whom he hath poured upon us abundantly, through Jesus Christ our Savior: that, being justified by his grace, we may be heirs, according to hope of life everlasting." Titus 3:5-7.

With the Methodists the Lord's Supper is merely a memorial of the passion and death of Jesus Christ. They receive bread and wine, imagining at the same time that Jesus comes to them in a spiritual manner.

Methodist Church

Imagination and emotion play a great part in Methodism, in contradistinction to Catholicism, where facts and reason are in perfect harmony with the revelations of God. Since Methodists reject Tradition and in contradistinction to the universal voice of early Christianity consider the Bible the sole source and rule of faith—that very Bible of which the Christians of the first half of the first century could have no knowledge, since it did not as yet exist—they cannot convince either themselves or others that they being of such recent date, constitute the Church which Jesus founded entirely without the Bible. He quoted the Old Testament; but He never even hinted to it that the Old Testament was the sole rule of faith. He did not quote the New Testament, because it was not as yet written. For it is well known that the New Testament was written after the ascension of Jesus Christ into heaven.

St. Paul gives this advice: "But we ought to give thanks to God always for you, brethren, beloved of God, for that God hath chosen you first fruits unto salvation, in sanctification of the spirit and faith of the truth: whereunto also he hath called you by our gospel, unto the purchasing of the glory of our Lord Jesus Christ. Therefore, brethren stand fast; and *hold the traditions which you have learned, whether by word or by our epistle.*" 2 Thess. 2:12-14.

The following are the principal Methodist bodies:

The Methodist Episcopal Church. It was organized at the "Christmas Conference" at Baltimore,

1784. Asbury was unanimously elected as *superintendent*, which name was changed to *bishop* in 1788. Episcopal Methodists are Wesleyan in doctrine and liturgy. M. E. is the abbreviation used to designate this branch of Methodism.

The Methodist Protestant Church was formed by some expelled Methodist Episcopal members and others who freely left the aforesaid denomination, because it would not extend governmental rights to laymen. It, too, started at Baltimore, Nov. 2, 1830. It has no bishops.

The Wesleyan Methodist Connection was the result of an anti-slavery movement at Utica, N. Y., 1843. It has neither bishops nor traveling preachers, and it does not permit its members to belong to secret societies.

The Congregational Methodists seceded from the Methodist Episcopal Church in 1852. They are Wesleyan in doctrine, and Congregational in polity.

The Free Methodist Church was organized by dissatisfied members of the M. E. Church, at Pekin, New York, 1860. They claimed that the M. E. Church had forsaken the original simplicity and spirituality of Methodism; that the preachers were at variance among themselves on doctrinal points; that the discipline was too lax; that the old simplicity of dress had given way to extravagance of apparel; that rented pews had taken the place of free seats; that choirs took the place of congregational singing; that members of secret societies were tolerated, etc. Instead of bishops, they have general superintendents.

Methodist Church

The use of intoxicating drinks and of tobacco, superfluous ornaments of dress, and joining secret societies are strictly forbidden among the Free Methodists. Direct witness of the Spirit (excitement); entire sanctification; eternal reward and punishment, are some of their express doctrines.

The New Congregational Methodists originated in Georgia, 1881, and are similar to the Congregational Methodists.

The Independent Methodists date back to 1810. They acknowledge no central government.

Other minor denominations among the Methodists are: Primitive Methodists; Bible Christians; United Methodist Free Churches; Welsh Calvinistic Methodists (Whitefield's harsh Calvinistic view of election and reprobation); African M. E. Zion Church; Union American M. E.; African M. E. Church; African Union Methodist Protestant Church; Zion Union Apostolic Church (founded in Virginia, 1869); Colored M. E. Church; etc.

With all its varied shades of doctrine and polity, and its many distinctive denominations, there are 11,900,000 Methodists in the world.

United Brethren in Christ

PHILIP WILLIAM OTTERBEIN, born in Germany, 1726, became a minister of the German Reformed Church and later on the main founder of the denomination known as United Brethren in Christ.

In his booklet, "The Church of the United Brethren in Christ," William M. Weekley, a U. B. bishop, writes: "Martin Boehm, Otterbein's earliest fellow-helper, was a member of the Mennonite Church. They first met at a great meeting held in Lancaster County, Pennsylvania, in 1767. As Otterbein listened to Boehm's sermon on Sabbath morning, he was deeply impressed by the simple, tender Scriptural message, and before the preacher could take his seat, Otterbein, quickened anew by the truth, and rejoicing in a new found fellowship, clasped Boehm in his arms and exclaimed, 'We are Brethren!' The effect upon the great audience was electrifying. Some were bathed in tears, while others shouted aloud for joy. All hearts seemed melted into one. There and then the United Brethren Church had its origin." Pages 3, 4.

Therefore, the United Brethren Church had its origin in Pennsylvania and not in the Holy Land, where the true Church originated; it was started in 1767 and is so many years separated from the time

United Brethren in Christ

when Jesus Christ, the founder of the Catholic Church, was born.

The first U. B. Conference was held in 1789. Philip W. Otterbein died as first bishop of the United Brethren Church in 1813. Bishop Boehm, the co-founder, had died one year before.

Bishops of the United Brethren Church are not ordained and are not made overseers for life, but are elected by the General Conference, which meets every four years and is composed of an equal number of ministerial and lay delegates chosen by the annual conferences. The ministers are chosen, not sent. In polity this denomination is similar to the Methodist Episcopal Church, i. e., it presents a fusion of the episcopal, presbyterian and congregational systems. It has a defined creed, a confession of faith, which, however, lacks precision. For example, instead of saying: "We believe in one God, in Whom there are three distinct persons, the Father, the Son and the Holy Ghost," they say: "We believe in the only true God, the Father, the Son and the Holy Ghost equal in essence or being with the Father and the Son."

In their first article of faith they maintain that the Bible is "the only rule and guide in faith and practice." By what the first Christians, who lived before the New Testament was written, were ruled and guided is not even alluded to.

Jesus never said that the Holy Bible (of which that part which we call the New Testament did not as yet exist when He lived on earth visibly), should be the only rule and guide in faith and practice; but we read in the same Holy Bible that Jesus said to His eleven Apostles shortly before He ascended into heaven: "All power is given to me in heaven and in earth. Going, therefore, teach ye all nations: baptizing them in the name of the Father, and of the Son, and of the Holy Ghost. Teaching them to observe all things whatsoever I have commanded you: and behold I am with you all days, even to the consummation of the world." Matt. 28:18-20.

Differing with the true Church, which always believed in seven Sacraments, the United Brethren believe in two only, viz: Baptism and the Lord's Supper; "but the mode of baptism and the manner of observing the Lord's Supper are always to be left to the judgment and understanding of each individual. Also, the baptism of children shall be left to the judgment of believing parents." Confession of Faith, No. 7.

They say: "We believe that penitent sinners are justified before God, only by faith in our Lord Jesus Christ, and not by works; yet good works in Christ are acceptable to God, and spring out of a true and living faith." No. 9. The Apostle St. James, a kinsman of our Lord, teaches a different doctrine. His is the teaching of the true Church. He writes: "What shall it profit, my brethren, if a man say he hath faith, but hath not works? Shall faith be able to save him? And if a brother or sister be naked, and want daily food: And one of you say to them: Go in peace, be ye warmed and filled; yet give them not those things that are necessary for the body, what shall it profit?

So faith also, if it have not works, is dead in itself. But some man will say: Thou hast faith, and I have works: shew me thy faith without works; and I will shew thee, by works, my faith. Thou believest that there is one God. Thou dost well: the devils also believe and tremble. But wilt thou know, O vain man, that faith without works is dead? Was not Abraham our father justified by works, offering up Isaac, his son, upon the altar? Seest thou, that faith did co-operate with his works: and by works faith was made perfect? And the Scripture was fulfilled, saying: Abraham believed God, and it was reputed to him to justice, and he was called the friend of God. Do you see that by works a man is justified; and not by faith only? And in like manner also Rahab, the harlot, was not she justified by works, receiving the messengers, and sending them out another way? For even as the body without the spirit is dead; so also faith without works is dead." James 2:14-26.

Though the United Brethren claim that the Holy Bible is the only rule and guide in faith and practice, nevertheless, they hold the tradition of keeping holy the Sunday instead of Saturday. They profess: "We believe that the Christian Sabbath (Sunday) is divinely appointed; that it is commemorative of our Lord's resurrection from the grave, and is an emblem of our eternal rest; that it is essential to the welfare of the civil community, and to the permanence and growth of the Christian Church, and that it should be reverently observed as a day of holy rest and of social and public worship." No. 12.

192 Christian Denominations

The main literary organ of the U. B. Church is "The Religious Telescope." In consequence of a schism, which occurred in 1889 in connection with the revision of the Confession of Faith and the constitution, there are today two distinct bodies of United Brethren. A small minority continued to stand by the "Old Constitution" with its prohibition attitude on the liquor question, secret societies, and war. In the United States there are 395,885 United Brethren.

Questions on the Text.

1. Who were the Moravians or Bohemian Brethren?
2. Who is the founder of the Quakers?
3. What do they mean by "Inner Lights?"
4. What misinterpretation do they give to our Savior's words on the cross: "It is consummated?"
5. Who started the Methodist Church?
6. In what year was it founded?
7. In what does the Methodist teaching on Baptism differ from that of the Catholic Church?
8. What does St. Paul say about Tradition?
9. Who was Philip William Otterbein?
10. When did the United Brethren Church originate?
11. Even before the New Testament was written what did Jesus command His Apostles and their successors to do?
12. Did Jesus and His Apostles ever hold that the Bible is the sole rule of Faith?
13. What has St. James to say on faith without good works?
14. What do the United Brethren hold concerning Sunday?

Adventists

THERE are six Protestant sects of Adventists in this country: "Evangelical Adventists," "Advent Christians," "Seventh Day Adventists," "Church of God," "Life and Advent Union," and "Age-to-come Adventists."

Their common belief is that Jesus Christ will speedily come and personally commence His much mooted hypothetical Millennium. Moreover, they agree in rejecting infant baptism, thus depriving children of the possibility of entering the kingdom of God; for "unless a man be born again of water and the Holy Ghost, he cannot enter into the kingdom of God." St. John 3:5. Adventists baptize adults by immersion.

The Evangelical Adventists date back their origin to William Miller (1781–1849), who, after a close but idiosyncratic study of the Biblical prophecies, announced that the end of the world would come in 1843. Of course, it did not come. Snow, his disciple, fixed the date for Oct. 22, 1844. But happily that day and year passed without the dread catastrophe. In 1845 these visionaries organized under the name of Evangelical Adventists. They believe that all will rise on Judgment Day: the just to reign with Christ during the Millennium and later on with Him in heaven; the wicked will be condemned to hell. Membership, 1,147.

The Advent Christians, founded in 1861, maintain that the souls of the dead slumber and remain unconscious till Christ comes again. They assert that Christ will annihilate the wicked, whereas the just will live forever. Evidently, they never grasped the meaning of the following words of Jesus Christ: *"And these* (the wicked) *shall go into everlasting punishment: but the just, into life everlasting."* St. Matt. 25:46. In order to show what Christ meant by *everlasting punishment*, I shall quote His own words: *"Depart from me, you cursed, into everlasting fire which was prepared for the devil and his angels."* St. Matt. 25:41. When the wicked go into everlasting punishment, they go down living and conscious into the everlasting, never-ending flames of hell. This is Bible truth; the teaching of the God-man Jesus Christ. According to the census report the Advent Christians have 30,975 members.

The Seventh Day Adventists celebrate the seventh day of the week instead of Sunday. They teach the utter annihilation of the wicked on Judgment Day, a doctrine, as we saw in the preceding paragraph, evidently contrary to the teaching of Christ. Mrs. E. G. White is their presumptuous interpreter of the prophecies of the Bible. They organized in 1845. Their number in 1922 was 82,287.

The Church of God as a body dates back to 1865 and is made up of such members of the Seventh Day Adventists as refuse to acknowledge the supposed prophetic gift of Mrs. White and the forced application of Apocalypse 12:11-17, to the United States of America. The history of this sect is like that of other heretics in the beginning they burn with zeal for their pet theory which gradually dwindles into nothingness.

The Life and Advent Union was started in 1848, but not fully organized until 1860. Members of this sect concede eternal rest to the damned by asserting that the wicked will sleep forever. It is a dreamy religion with a membership of 3,800.

The Age-to-come Adventists organized in 1851. They believe that the human soul is material and slumbers in the grave until the coming of Christ on Judgment Day, when the just receive life from Jesus Christ and the sleepy souls of the wicked pass out of existence. This absurd teaching is not only contrary to what Jesus plainly taught concerning the everlasting punishment of the wicked, but it is also diametrically opposed to sound philosophy. The human soul, God's image and likeness, will exist forever and forever, conscious of its being. There are 146,177 Adventists in the United States.

Christian Catholic Church of Zion

Dowieites

※※※

JOHN ALEXANDER DOWIE was born in Edinburgh, Scotland, in 1847. In order to get reliable information concerning this man, after whom the Dowieites are named, I wrote a letter of inquiry to his successor, W. G. Voliva, who promptly ordered his ecclesiastical secretary to furnish me the desired information by answering my letter and liberally forwarding some of their more important literature. The letter written, July 25, 1911, by G. L. Carey, General Ecclesiastical Secretary of Zion City, Ill., offers the following information.

"Dr. Dowie who was born in Edinburgh, Scotland, and who was brought up in Australia, and entered the Christian ministry in that country, doing a large amount of work, came to America, landing at San Francisco on June 7, 1888.

"After working actively in many states along the Western coast preaching the Gospel of the Kingdom, and being used of God in the healing of many persons, he arrived in Chicago in July, 1890, taking up his residence in Evanston.

"In the city of Chicago, he labored for a number of years with great success, though, at first, he had many difficulties and the work assumed only small dimensions. After reaching a certain point, however, before which, I might say, he had been severely tempted to give up the work, the tide of victory came and from that time on the work grew with great strides.

"Great crowds of people were attracted to him, and many wonderful healings took place; and his name became a household one throughout the civilized world.

"Regarding his preaching, I might say that Dr. Dowie 'rung the changes' on repentance, calling upon men and women to forsake all sin and the customs of the world which were, in any way, injurious to man.

"Very prominent in his teaching was the subject of Divine Healing that made him so renowned. His claim was that the Holy Scriptures taught that men must forsake all earthly physicians, and that God alone is the Healer of His people.

"He stood very strongly for a holy Church. He opposed many things which he found existed in the churches, and it was his opposition to these things that made him many enemies.

"Dr. Dowie, however, was a man who was not only bold on the platform concerning the positions which he took, but those who knew him found that he was a man with a great heart of love; so that whilst he had many enemies, he had many friends amongst those who were not affiliated with him in church life.

"For many years, Dr. Dowie had the vision of a Zion City; and when the opportune time arrived, he took his first step in realizing this, his cherished ambition, and Zion City was inaugurated really when the portion of ground known as 'The Temple Site' was dedicated on July 14, 1901.

"Zion City was founded for God's people and was intended to be an illustration of applied Christianity. The lease which Dr. Dowie adopted for persons taking up residence and other properties here was a unique one, forbidding alcohol, tobacco, theatres, secret societies, swine and swine's flesh, and many other things.

"Many people came here and much money was poured into Zion's coffers, and great progress was made and a wonderful city established. Troublesome times, however, came along, owing to mismanagement; and then Dr. Dowie took sick and passed away in 1907; but the man, Wilbur Glenn Voliva, whom Dr. Dowie had chosen to be his successor, had already been recalled by him from Australia to take up the reins.

"General Overseer Voliva has gone right ahead with the work of standing for the same truths and principles as Dr. Dowie stood for. It is true he has met with some opposition, but this opposition is daily weakening, and there is no doubt as to the outcome.

"Mr. Voliva has had great success during the last three years since he commenced to purchase back from the Receiver of the Zion Estate various properties in the city, culminating with the purchase from the Receiver of the remainder of the estate.

"The preaching of Zion has, for its keynote, the Kingdom of God; and Zion City is intended to be an exemplification, as far as it is possible to make it, of the Kingdom of God on earth. It is only a beginning, it is true, but we believe it is a beginning." So far the letter.

Alexander Dowie called his religious organization "The Christian Catholic Apostolic Church," and, after meeting with many disappointments among his adherents, he died March 9, 1907. W. G. Voliva succeeded him, whilst the Dowieites were divided into two factions; some stubbornly refusing to acknowledge Voliva as General Overseer of Zion City, others preferring his executive abilities to those of the Dowie family.

The Dowieites believe in the Blessed Trinity. They adore Jesus Christ and venerate the Bible as the inspired book of God. Dowieites admit that hell fire is, as Christ says, everlasting. They believe that good works are necessary as well as faith. The following extract from Voliva's "Leaves of Healing," July 23, 1911, will show this: "The Apostle says that a fountain cannot send forth at one time, both sweet and bitter water. God does not like any 'halfway' service. When you come to this altar, you put your whole being down there—your all: your spirit, your soul, your body, your memory—everything that is precious to you, that is good for something—God does not want any trash, nor any whiskey, nor any tobacco. If a man has a whiskey store, or a tobacco store, he does not consecrate it to God; he cannot, for God will not accept it. God wants a pure, holy sacrifice: a clean man." Since Dowieites presume that it is wrong to have a tobacco store, they cannot consecrate it to God:

they have to stay out of that business. The Lord has nowhere forbidden the traffic of either whiskey or tobacco. The abuse, however, of either article is a sin against the fifth Commandment: "Thou shalt not kill."

In 1896, when Dowie was trying to form his new church, he made the following assertion concerning baptism: "I am a firm believer in Baptism as essential to a full and perfect Obedience, but if you desire to make Baptism a test of Christian Fellowship, I decline to be in such a Church, because I was a Christian before I was immersed."—A Voice from Zion. Dowieites are baptized by threefold immersion. They do not believe that a person becomes a child of God by baptism, but hold, on the contrary that one must be a child of God previous to immersion. Here they are at variance with the saying of Jesus Christ: "Amen, amen, I say to thee, unless a man be born again of water and the Holy Ghost, he cannot *enter* into the kingdom of God." St. John 3:5. In the Acts we read: "Do penance, and be baptized every one of you in the name of Jesus Christ *for the remissions of your sins.*" Acts 2:38. Before original sin and other mortal sins are remitted, a person cannot be called a child of God.

Dowieites have communion services in memory of the Last Supper, during which they receive bread and wine; and whilst they partake of this, they implore God that this eating may result in a spiritual communion and partaking of the Blood of Christ. Their notion of the Blessed Eucharist is about as hazy as can be imagined, whereas the words of Jesus are as plain as they can be: *"This is my body. This is my blood."*

Dowie once said: "There can never be a new church, unless it be a false church. That which is true with regard to Church organization is not new; and that which is new is not true." A Voice from Zion, P. 43. On the next page he maintains: "The Church of God in each generation must be a Building whole and complete in itself, and must be such a Building today in the nineteenth century, as it was nineteen centuries ago." Nineteen centuries ago, as may be seen from the Testimony of Well Known Writers of the First Five Centuries, in this very book, Christians believed in the uninterrupted continuation of the Church which Jesus founded; they believed in the necessity of baptism for the forgiveness of sins as a means of becoming a true Christian; they professed their belief in the Real Presence and in fact in all the teachings which the members of that same Church believe and practice today. The Church of "Primitive Christianity," to which Dowieites are fond to refer, continues throughout all ages, teaching and following everywhere the same.

Dowie's associate, Mr. Calverly, a former Methodist, made this remark anent Christianity: "What we have left has been handed down principally from the Apostate Roman Catholic Church—a miserable institution." Suffice it to add that Calverly's "miserable institution" is in no way the real Roman Catholic Church, but simply a creation of his deeply prejudiced mind; but it is true that what is left of Christianity, and thanks to God all is left of it, has been handed down and is being handed down by the Roman Catholic Church.

As far as I can gather from his writings and sermons, Dowie spoke respectfully of the Catholic Church and its means of salvation. Speaking on St. John 20:23 he remarks: "I know that some may think immediately that this approaches perilously near to Rome. I do not care a pin; if the Roman Catholic Church has a truth I am going to say it, and I do not care who takes the other side." A Voice from Zion, P. 11. It is a pity that Dowie did not know much about the Catholic Church; otherwise he would have said the truths of this Church and led his people into it. He failed to do it. Therefore, he was either ignorant of what the Catholic Church teaches or he was not sincere in his statement.

Every month the Dowieites are supposed to come to their temple and make a general confession of repentance and of faith. On such occasions Dowie would ask them: "Do you mean it?" Upon the answer: "I do mean it," he would assure them that their sins were forgiven. He was in no way a legitimate successor of the Apostles, and therefore he had absolutely no right to assure them of a thing of which he himself knew nothing. To the Apostles and their rightful successors was given the power to forgive and to retain sins. Jesus, addressing His Apostles, said to them: *"Receive ye the Holy Ghost. Whose sins you shall forgive, they are forgiven them; and whose sins you shall retain, they are retained."* St. John 20:22, 23.

The government of Dowie's new church is monarchical; and the members love to call it The Kingdom Movement of Zion. We have no adverse criticism to offer on their pious endeavor to keep other denominations out of their city.

Moreover, we add that it is pleasing to God to pray for the recovery of the sick; but it is displeasing to Him to refuse to make use of the medicinal helps which He has prepared for us in nature, of which He Himself is the author. It is wrong, anti-biblical and diametrically opposed to God's own verdict, to say that it is sinful to have recourse to a physician. Dowieites believe that God inspired the writers of the Bible. In the Bible we read: "Honor the physician for the need thou hast for him; for the most High hath created him. For all healing is from God, and he shall receive gifts of the king. The skill of the physician shall lift up his head, and in the sight of great men he shall be praised. The most High hath created medicines out of the earth, and a wise man will not abhor them. Was not bitter water made sweet with wood? The virtue of these things is come to the knowledge of men, and the most High hath given knowledge to men, that he may be honored in his wonders. By these he shall cure and allay their pains, and of these apothecary shall make sweet confections, and shall make up ointments of health, and of his works there shall be no end. For the peace of God is over all the face of the earth. My son, in thy sickness neglect not thyself, but pray to the Lord, and he shall heal thee. Turn away from sin and order thy hands aright, and cleanse thy heart from all offence. Give a sweet savor, and a memorial of fine flour, and make a fat offering, and *then give place to the physician.* For the Lord created him; and let him not depart from thee, for his works are necessary. For there is a time when thou must fall into their hands; and they shall beseech the Lord, that he would prosper what they give for ease and remedy, for their conversation. He that sinneth in the sight of his Maker, shall fall into the hands of the physician." Ecclesiasticus 38:1-15.

Though the Dowieites, as well as the Eddyists, or "Christian Scientists," refuse medical aid, they must not be confounded with the latter. Dowieites are Christians; "Christian Scientists" are not. Dowieites *hope that God cure* them; Eddyists *pretend to cure* by sheer mental effort. There is an essential difference between Faith-Cure and Mental Healing. Dowieites adore Jesus Christ, Eddyists do not; they deny His divinity. Dowieites believe in the necessity of penance and good works in order to gain heaven; Eddyists deny sin, death, hell, and all consequences of sin. Dowieites believe that God is the Creator of Heaven and earth; Eddyists maintain that everything is a part of God or, to use their own language, that God is All in all, that He is the only Mind.

The Dowieites in general are well-meaning people. They pride themselves on belonging to the "Christian Catholic Church." May God grant them the grace really to become members of the Christian Catholic Church which Jesus founded not in Zion

Christian Catholic Church of Zion 205

City, but in Palestine some nineteen hundred years ago, and which still exists as He Himself foretold, and which is none other than the Catholic Church of which the Pope at Rome and not the Overseer at Zion City is the supreme visible head.

According to the Statistics of 1911 as given in the World Almanac, the membership of this sect is 5,865; though the Dowieites themselves claim many more adherents.

Salvation Army

SALVATIONISTS

WILLIAM BOOTH and his wife Catherine, both preachers of the Methodist New Connection, since 1865, devoted a great deal of time to the noble work of instructing and bettering the inhabitants of the lowest slums in London, thus trying to lead all classes of profligates, thieves, drunkards, libertines and vagabonds to a better life. Moreover, they preached to all who cared to listen to them. They went from city to city and succeeded in getting co-laborers and gradually established small societies, which they called "Christian Mission." In 1878 William Booth changed the name of "Christian Mission" to that of "Salvation Army." By that time he and his wife had over a hundred co-laborers. They made converts among the classes mentioned and also among other people who were not affiliated with any particular church organization.

The head of this imitative military band is called General. In fact, the military idea is carried out in their uniforms, discipline, titles and services. Their local associations are called "corps," their ministers, both men and women, "officers," their public prayers "knee drills," their public religious exercises "skirmishes," etc. We see them in cities with their banners, making all kinds of noise with drums and cymbals and shouting "hallelujah." Whilst one of them speaks, the others applaud, and women wave their handkerchiefs. In connection with some well-meant address, some of them will step out to tell the story of their conversion. Though the story is often told in the most uncouth manner, the purpose of it all is to give glory to Christ, who saved them, and induce other similar sinners to quit sin and lead a better life.

As might be expected, many of the enthusiastic converts relapse after a short time, and great scandals occur; for which, however, the Salvation Army ought not to be blamed. Some remain firm in their good resolutions and henceforth lead an honest life. Imitating the Catholic Brothers and Sisters of benevolent institutions, the Salvation Army helps to feed the hungry and to take care of the needy.

Members of the Salvation Army are not known as church-goers, on the contrary, they prefer to parade on the public streets. Mohammedans and heathens, as well as Christians, can become members of the Salvation Army without changing their creed. The Salvationists do not even consider baptism and Holy Eucharist in any way necessary for salvation. In their meetings doctrinal disputes are to be avoided; but all are supposed to believe that mankind was totally corrupted by the fall of Adam; that contrition and penance are necessary: that justification is accomplished solely through the belief in the atoning blood and merits of Jesus Christ and the witness of the Holy Ghost; that all mankind will be judged on the last day; that heaven is the eternal reward of those who are saved, and that hell is the eternal punishment for those who are lost.

The Salvation Army wisely makes no pretense of being the one true Church.

In the United States this denomination counts at present 74,768 adherents divided into two bodies, the Salvation Army established by Booth and the American Salvation Army, which seceded from the former in 1882 under Moore. The original organization is primarily philanthropic, the latter primarily religious.

Mormons

Church of Jesus Christ of Latter-Day Saints

JOSEPH SMITH, born in Sharon township, Windsor Co., Vermont, Dec. 23, 1805, is the founder of Mormonism. He claimed that a heavenly messenger by the name of Moroni appeared to him on the night of Sept. 21, 1823, who revealed to him three times that a complete record written upon gold plates with two transparent stones in silver bows like spectacles, by means of which the ancient record could be read, were deposited in the earth, in a hill (which was shown him), near Manchester, Ontario Co., New York. He, moreover, states that this angel placed these records of gold and the stone spectacles called Urim and Thummim, into his hands on Sept. 22, 1827. Sitting behind a blanket to shield these records from profane eyes, the two stones upon his nose, Joseph Smith, the visionary (so he says), began to read these records, the wonderful Book of Mormon. What Joseph Smith read by means of stone spectacles, Oliver Cowdery wrote down. Joseph Smith had never learned to read or write well, for his schooling had been somewhat neglected.

The "Book of Mormon" was published in 1830. It contains a peculiar Testimony of Three Witnesses, who claim that they saw the plates. Since I have the book before me, as I write, I quote a few sentences of the testimony of the three witnesses: "And we also testify that we have seen the engravings which are upon the plates; and they have been shewn unto us by the power of God, and not of man. And we declare with words of soberness, that an angel of God came down from heaven, and he brought and laid before our eyes, that we beheld and saw the plates, and the engravings thereon." The names signed are: Oliver Cowdery, David Whitmer, Martin Harris. Several years afterwards all *these three witnesses* quarrelled with Smith, renounced Mormonism and *declared that their testimony in the Book of Mormon is false*. When Oliver Cowdery, David Whitmer and Martin Harris admitted the falsity of their testimony in the Book of Mormon, eight other witnesses with equal soberness asserted that they saw the plates from which Joseph Smith translated by the aid of stone spectacles.

Nobody else ever saw these golden plates. The imposition is very palpable. Although repeatedly and loudly demanded, these supposed golden plates have never been forthcoming. Even among the Mormon leaders the knowledge of those fabulous plates and wonderful stone spectacles is at most traditional.

Though his neighbors witnessed against Joseph Smith, and many held him up to ridicule, he succeeded in organizing his church at Fayette, N. Y., April 6, 1830, under the pretentious name of *Church of Jesus Christ of Latter Day Saints*. He himself

Mormons

was accepted by his disciples as their first elder, and was subsequently honored by them as prophet and revelator. In 1843, when his lawful wife was jealous, because of his cohabiting with other women, Joseph Smith had another vision which resulted in establishing polygamy, which he taught and practiced. Others followed his example. This public scandal caused the trouble at Nauvoo, Ill., between the Mormon militia and the U. S. soldiers. The governor of the state persuaded the two Smiths, Joseph and Hyrum to surrender and stand a trial. But whilst they were in prison at Carthage, a mob overpowered the guards and shot and killed Hyrum Smith instantly. Joseph Smith used his revolver on the mob, but when his charges were exhausted in his attempt to escape, he was shot and fell to the ground dead, June 27, 1844. Thus died the founder of Mormonism, the advocate of polygamy.

Soon after, Brigham Young was chosen first president of the Mormons. In 1845 the Illinois legislature repealed the Nauvoo charter. A year later Brigham Young went west and finally arrived in Salt Lake Valley, July 24, 1847. Salt Lake City was founded by the Mormons that same year. It became their lasting home. Brigham Young was not only their spiritual leader, but upon the acknowledged petition sent to President Millard Fillmore, he became their rightful governor, 1850. The practice of polygamy has brought them repeatedly into conflict with the laws of the land.

It may seem strange to the reader that the Book

of Mormon forbids polygamy, whereas the founder of Mormonism practiced it to such an extent that sixteen women testified against him on account of this vice. In the book of Jacob (the third book in the Book of Mormon) chapter 3, V. 27, we read as follows: "Wherefore, my brethren, hear me and hearken to the word of the Lord; for there shall not any man among you have save it be one wife; and concubines he shall have none." Joseph Smith, in spite of this, establishes polygamy as though it were perfectly in harmony with the will of God.

The Mormons have a wrong conception of the fall of man. They believe: "Adam fell that men might be; and men are, that they might have joy." 2 Nephi, 2:25. In other words, they imagine that Adam's sin was that of lust. Holy Scripture says plainly: "And the woman saw that the tree was good to eat, and fair to the eyes, and delightful to behold: and she took of the fruit thereof, and did eat, and gave to her husband who did eat." Gen. 3:6.

They believe in the necessity of baptism. "And now, if the Lamb of God, he being holy, should have need to be baptized by water, to fulfill all righteousness, O then, how much more need have we, being unholy, to be baptized, yea, even by water." 2 Nephi, Chap. 31, V. 5. Moreover, they believe in the incarnation of the Son of God. "And behold, he shall be born of Mary, at Jerusalem (?) which is in the land of our forefathers, she being a virgin, a precious and chosen vessel, who shall be overshadowed, and conceive by the power of the Holy Ghost, and bring forth a son, yea, even the Son of God." Alma, Chap. 7, V. 10.

Mormons believe in the Blessed Trinity as is very plainly seen from different passages in the Book of Mormon; they believe, too, that Jesus Christ is the Son of God; that all men through the atonement of Jesus Christ may be saved by obedience to the laws and ordinances of the Gospel. By ordinances of the Gospel they understand: Faith in the Lord Jesus Christ; Baptism by immersion for the remission of sins; Repentance, and Laying on of hands for the gift of the Holy Ghost.

According to Elder M. F. Cowley, in his book, "Cowley's Talks On Doctrine," page 83: "The Latter Day Saints regard our Heavenly Father as possessing an actual tabernacle of flesh and bones (not blood), and that in His image man is created." We know by the authority of St. John that Jesus said: "God is a spirit." St. John 4:24. On another occasion Jesus said: "A spirit hath not flesh and bones." St. Luke 24:39. The Mormon flesh and bone theory of God is wrong; for God is a spirit and a spirit has not flesh and bones.

"As Latter Day Saints we believe that all creation existed spiritually before the physical organism was brought into existence." Cowley's Talks on Doctrine, P. 154. They base this theory upon Genesis 1:24, by confounding spiritual existence with kinds of creatures. And God said: "Let the earth bring forth the living creature in its kind, cattle and creeping things, and beasts of the earth, according to their kinds. And it was so done." Gen. 1:24.

On marriage Mormons hold this opinion: "We believe that God ordained the union of the sexes in marriage, not only for time but for all eternity." Cowley's Talks on Doctrine, P. 274.

Jesus teaches a different doctrine. When the Sadducees, trying to argue against the resurrection, brought the example of one woman who had been successively married to seven brothers and then died, they asked Jesus: "At the resurrection, therefore, whose wife of the seven shall she be? for they all had her. And Jesus answering, said to them: You err, not knowing the Scriptures, nor the power of God. For in the resurrection they shall neither marry nor be married; but shall be as the angels of God in heaven." Matt. 22:28-30.

Abortion and other practices of the race suicide category scarcely ever occur among the Mormons. As a rule they have large families. "Because the children are numerous they are not weaker, but usually stronger in body and intellect than in communities where the blighting curse of a reprehensible modern custom prevails. The wives of men thus taught and convinced of the sacredness of their procreative functions are healthier and happier in the home than are wives and mothers in other communities." Cowley's Talks on Doctrine, P. 276.

Mormons dream of a happy Millennium when the Savior will visibly dwell and reign on earth in peace and universal happiness for one thousand years at

Zion, the holy city of Jerusalem. He will put His feet on Mount Olivet, "and the mount will cleave in twain." The Jews will convert to Jesus and will be baptized for the remission of their sins.

The total number of Mormons, or Latter Day Saints is about 606,561.

Universalists

JAMES RELLY, an associate of Whitefield in preaching Calvinistic Methodism, gradually, about 1750, exchanged his severe views of predestination for the other extreme of ultimate salvation for all, for the good and bad alike. He succeeded in gathering a congregation of adherents in England.

One of his preachers, *John Murray,* came to America in 1770 and began to preach Relly's tenets in Boston. All who adopted this extremely optimistic view were called Universalists. The sect was organized on this continent in 1785. John Murray died 1815.

Universalists uniformly believe that ultimately all mankind will be saved. Some of them maintain that all go straight to heaven as soon as they die; others hold that the wicked will be punished for a while, but that none will be punished everlastingly. They do not believe in the existence of hell. Of Jesus they speak as of a man divinely sent and gifted with spirit and power above all other created intelligences; they regard Him as a superior being in whom God displayed the brightness of His glory. They deny the doctrine of the Blessed Trinity and thus the Godhead of Jesus Christ. When they speak of His divinity, they simply mean that He was divinely sent and that God in a special way manifested Himself in Him. In this sense they admit His "divinity," but they flatly deny His "Godhead." In brief, they do not believe that He is God. The denial of the "Godhead" of Jesus Christ is blasphemous. Jesus is God and proved it by His miracles.

Whenever the utterances of Christ are too plainly opposed to their views they resort to quibbling. If they actually believe that Jesus "is gifted with spirit and power above all intelligence," they ought to admit the truth of His statements. Now Jesus says that on the last judgment day the King "shall say to them also that shall be on his left hand: Depart from me, you cursed, into *everlasting fire* which was prepared for the devil and his angels." St. Matt. 25:41. He plainly states that the punishment will last as long as the reward; for He says: "And these (the wicked) shall go into *everlasting punishment;* but the just into *live everlasting.*" St. Matt. 25:46.

The Catholic Church teaches that there is a chance of salvation for all, even for the greatest sinners, if they co-operate with the grace of God and thus sincerely convert, if they do what God wants them to do, and becoming thus reconciled with Him die in the state of sanctifying grace. But those who die in mortal sin, are lost forever. Death cuts off for them the opportunity of salvation. A mortal sin is a willful transgression of the law of God in an important matter. Full knowledge of the evil, the full consent of the will, and an important matter in which the sinner offends, is necessary to constitute such a mortal sin. If a person repents of this sin, God as a kind Father, is willing to forgive; but if the sinner does not repent, he remains in the malice of the evil and dies as an enemy of God. It stands to reason that God does not reward His enemies with everlasting happiness in heaven.

Their moral persuasion of leading people away from sin and to the practice of virtue is curtly given in the "Profession of Faith," which was adopted at Winchester, N. H., 1803, and in which we read: "We believe that holiness and true happiness are inseparably connected, and that believers ought to be careful to maintain order and practice good works; for these things are good and profitable unto men." Article 3.

Universalists, of course, have not a shadow of a claim to be the Church which Jesus founded; though they are not quite so un-Christian as the Unitarians, with whom they also differ in holding at least some sort of supernatural inspiration of the Bible.

The membership is 54,957.

Unitarians

THE first congregation of Unitarians was gathered in London about the year 1645 by John Biddle. He is called the "Father of English Unitarianism." Church history shows that individuals and temporary sects with tendencies similar to the Unitarians appeared spasmodically in the course of the Christian era.

"The founder of the present organized body of English Unitarians was the Rev. Theophilus Linsley, who left the Church of England and gathered a Unitarian congregation in Essex Street, London, in 1774, which included many noted people. He was followed the next year by Dr. Joseph Priestly, famous as a man of science, and especially as the discoverer of oxygen. The law at that time held the denial of the Trinity to be blasphemy, and it was not until 1813 that Unitarians were placed on a level with other Dissenters." W. H. Lyon, A Study of the Sects.

The theology of the Unitarian sect is of a negative character and consists mainly in a denial of Christian doctrines and practices. Unitarians reject the Doctrine of the Blessed Trinity: the dogma of three persons in one God. Moreover, they deny the divinity of Jesus Christ, His supernatural birth, His vicarious atonement, and the institution of His saving sacraments. Original sin and eternal punishment are not admitted by them. In short, Unitarianism is simply a negation of Christianity. They take from the Bible what suits them and question the authenticity of such passages as do not agree with their opinions. Though esteeming the Bible as a masterpiece of literature, they deny its divine inspiration.

They deny all sacraments, but in spite of this generally adhere to the rite of infant baptism, and hold the Lord's Supper, which they have in their churches as merely commemorative of the death of Christ, as that of a martyr and as expressive of spiritual communion with Him.

Unitarians claim to be Christians and maintain that Christ is their model man. But I maintain all those who deny the divinity of Christ, who deny that He is God, have no right to the name of Christian.

The prophets inspired by God had foretold that God would redeem the world. They designated Jesus Christ, the Son of the Virgin, whose birthplace would be Bethlehem, as the redeemer.

Jesus proved His divinity by His miracles, His prophecies, His repeated testimony, and especially by His own resurrection from the dead which He had foretold. Therefore, Jesus is God. That He publicly claimed to be the Son of God was so well known that His enemies used this declaration as an argument against Him, to condemn Him to the cross. "Again the high priest asked him: Art thou the Christ the Son of the blessed God? And Jesus said to him: I am." St. Mark. 14:61, 62. Read the accounts of the passion of Jesus as recorded in the last chapters of

Unitarians

the Gospel of Sts. Matthew, Mark, Luke and John.

From the time of Christ unto the present day the enemies of Christ have denied His divinity. They should not arrogate to themselves the name of Christian. We know that Unitarian literature is directed against Christ's divinity.

Unitarianism in its dogmatic tenets is no more Christian than Judaism, Mohammedanism or heathenism. In practice they may resemble the Christians more than heathens generally do. No Christian can at the same time be a Unitarian.

In this country the Unitarians are credited with an affiliated membership of only 60,152 but there are, alas, millions of nominal Christians of their type.

Church of the New Jerusalem

EMANUEL SWEDENBORG, born Jan. 29, 1688, the son of a Swedish Lutheran bishop, a scholar of considerable eminence and author of many philosophical, mathematical and exegetical works, is the founder of the "Church of the New Jerusalem." He expects us to believe that God in a solemn manner had destined him to introduce a new and permanent era of Christianity, that the heavens had opened to his gaze and the mysteries of God were unfolded to him, and many other wonderful things.

Swedenborg claims that the New Jerusalem, the kingdom of God on earth, commenced on June 19, 1770, on the very day on which he had completed his literary work, "True Christian Religion; containing the Universal Theology of the New Church;" and that upon its completion Jesus Christ sent out His Apostles through the entire spiritual world to announce to the spirits the glad tidings that henceforth God's kingdom was to remain forever and ever.

Thus the Church of the New Jerusalem was established in 1770, upon the mere, albeit perhaps honest, presumption of the visionary Emanuel Swedenborg.

In his alleged visit to the spirit-world he found Luther not as yet converted from the wrong doctrine on justification and consequently still barred from heaven, and Calvin, he saw in hell on account of his stubborn refusal to abandon his false predestination theory. This is given in his book "True Religion, etc." Vol. 2, P. 553 sequ.

Swedenborg does not hold the Lutheran doctrine of justification by faith alone, but he insists upon the practice of charity, upon good works; neither does he in any way agree with Calvin on fatal predestination.

But he denies original sin, the necessity of redemption, the Blessed Trinity, and five of the Sacraments, retaining Baptism and the Eucharist.

In his interpretation of the Bible, or rather part of the Bible, for he does not believe in the Acts of the Apostles, nor in the letters of St. Paul, he ignores the literal sense and explains passage upon passage in an allegorical sense. His voluminous exegetical work is called "Arcana Coelestia." To give the reader a better knowledge of his mode of interpretation, I adduce a few quotations from the first volume of his "Coelestial Arcana." "1. That the Word of the Old Testament includes arcana of heaven, and that all its contents, to every particular regard the Lord, his heaven, the church, faith and the things relating to faith no man can conceive who only views it from the letter. For the letter, or literal sense, suggests only such things as respect the externals of the Jewish church, when, nevertheless, it everywhere contains internal things, which do not in the least appear in those externals except in a very few cases, where the Lord revealed and unfolded them to the apostles—as that sacrifice is significative of the Lord—and that the church of Canaan and Jerusalem are significative of heaven, on which account they are called the heavenly Canaan and Jerusalem—and that Paradise has a like signification. 2. But that all and every part of its contents, even to the most minute, not excepting the smallest jot and tittle, signify and involve spiritual and celestial things, is a truth to this day deeply hidden from the Christian world, in consequence of which little attention is paid to the Old Testament. This truth, however, might appear plainly from this single circumstance: that the Word being of the Lord, could not possibly be given without containing interiorly such things as relate to heaven, to the church, and to faith. For, if this be denied, how can it be called the Word of the Lord, or be said to have any life in it? From whence is its life but from these things which possess life, that is except from hence, that all things in it, both generally and particularly have relation to the Lord, who is the very Life Itself? Wherefore, whatsoever does not interiorly regard Him, does not live; nay, whatsoever expression in the Word does not involve Him or in its measure relate to Him, is not divine." Arcana Coelestia, Vol. 1; No. 1, 2.

Swedenborg goes to the extreme in his allegorical interpretation of Genesis; for here he entirely ignores and at least apparently denies the literal sense. He offers no proof for the correctness of his allegories except an appeal to a creation of his phantasy which he calls the "Most Ancient People" and tells us: "It was well known in the most Ancient Church."

"In the beginning God created Heaven, and earth." Gen. 1:1. By create Swedenborg understands to regenerate; by earth he denotes man, who was *void* of good, and *empty* of truth.

"And the earth was void and empty, and darkness was upon the face of the deep; and the Spirit of God moved over the waters." Gen. 1:2. Swedenborg offers this allegorical explanation: "The faces of the abyss (deep) are the lusts of the unregenerated man, and the falsities thence originating of which he consists and in which he is totally immersed." A. C., V. 1, No. 18.

"By the Spirit of God is meant the mercy of the Lord, which is said to move, or brood, as a hen broods over her eggs." A. C. P. 7; No. 19. From these few passages it becomes manifest that Swedenborg's interpretation may be very appropriately styled: An ingenious play of fancy.

His form of Baptism gives us a clue to his opinion on the Blessed Trinity. Members of the Church of New Jerusalem use this formulary: "I baptize thee into the name of the Lord Jesus Christ, who is Father, Son and Holy Ghost." This excludes three distinct persons and includes a threefold manifestation of one and the same person. Swedenborg and his adherents profess to believe in the Godhead of Jesus Christ. Jesus is God, the Eternal Truth. He said: "I will ask the Father, and *He* shall give you *another* Paraclete, that he may abide with you forever." St. John 14:16.

Hereby Jesus indicates that His Father is a person different from Himself, and the other Paraclete is neither the Father nor Himself, but a distinct third person. "But the Paraclete, the Holy Ghost, whom the Father will send in my name, he will teach you all things, and bring all things to your mind, whatsoever I shall have said to you." St. John 14:26.

The formulary used by the Swedenborgians is not scriptural; it is not the one that Jesus Himself has given us, "Going, therefore, *teach ye* all nations; baptizing them *in the name of the Father, and of the Son and of the Holy Ghost.*" St. Matt. 28:19.

Even if we admit that E. Swedenborg possessed great learning and well deserved fame, we cannot ignore the fact that his writings betray a lamentable ignorance of Church-History, of the early Fathers, and of the dogmas held the world over. This total ignorance of ecclesiastical and dogmatic history leads him to the gratuitous assertion that the Council of Nice fabricated a new and erroneous notion of the Trinity. His whole system of doctrines is dreamy and fully of inconsistencies.

Though the author and founder of the Church of the New Jerusalem is extremely sober and earnest, nevertheless, his writings contain abundant matter for amusement or ridicule.

That J. A. Moehler holds a similar opinion will appear from the subjoined passage:

"Swedenborg shows great pettiness, and even childishness, in making a sort of fire-work out of Holy Writ. In the spiritual world, says he, where the Bible is preserved in holy chests, in the sanctuary of the Temple, it is regarded with respect by the angels; (here the fire-work starts) and it is as radiant as a real star, and, at times, like the sun and its glimmering splendor forms the most magnificent rainbow! If anyone, with his hands or clothes, touch the Bible, he is immediately environed with a brilliant fire, and he appears as if standing in the midst of a star bathed in light!" Symbolism, 84.

Swedenborg died, March 29, 1772, at London, where he claimed to have received his doctrines from God. His death was owing to a stroke of apoplexy which had disabled him since 1771.

The World Almanac of 1922 divides the Swedenborgians into "General Convention" and "General Church" and gives the total membership of the Church of the New Jerusalem in this country as amounting to 7,085.

Church of Christ, Scientist

"Christian Science," or Eddyism

※

THE denomination which calls itself the *Church of Christ, Scientist,* but which is more properly styled *Eddyism* after its foundress, is neither Christian nor scientific in spite of the fact that it has come to be named Christian Science. It was founded in 1876 at Boston, Mass., by the late Mrs. Mary Baker Glover Patterson Eddy. Her maiden name was Baker; the other names she acquired by marrying Mr. Glover, then Mr. Patterson, from whom she was divorced and during whose lifetime she became the wife of Mr. Eddy.

The sum total of "Christian Science" tenets is contained in her book, which was published in 1875. It is called "Science and Health with Key to the Scriptures." From the contents of this book, as well as from the articles in the Christian Science Sentinel, the Christian Science Monitor, and other publications, we infer that the "Christian Scientists'" great hobby is "mental healing;" i.e., getting rid of the idea that there is really such a thing as matter, sickness, sin, and the consequences of the same.

"Christian Scientists" do not believe in the Blessed Trinity; they do not believe that there are three distinct persons in God. They deny the divinity of Jesus

Church of Christ, Scientist

Christ, whom they divide into two persons. Angels are not considered spirits among them, but only divine messages, instead of messengers. They deny the creation of man, the maternity of the Blessed Virgin Mary, the future resurrection of all men as well as the resurrection of Jesus Christ, ignoring on this topic both history and Holy Scripture. Original sin, death and hell are branded as delusions.

"Science and Health with Key to the Scriptures" contains the following sentence in the 169th Edition on page 140: "Man is neither young or old. He has neither birth nor death." On page 107 we read: "The sensation of sickness and sin exists only in belief;" and on page 172: "If God is admitted to be the only Mind and Life there ceases to be any opportunity for sin and death." "Christian Scientists" maintain that God is the only Mind and Life.

In a leaflet entitled: "The Real and the Unreal," the Christian Scientist S. J. Hanna writes: "We wish it distinctly understood that our text-book does not treat sin, sickness and death lightly, as some seem to think. On the contrary, it teaches that, humanly speaking, they are to be overcome and destroyed as Jesus and his disciples overcame and destroyed them. It teaches that it was a solemn mission of Jesus and his disciples to prove the *unreality* of sin, sickness and *death* by destroying them, and that it is the duty of Jesus' followers in all ages to strive to learn the divine law by virtue of which he did this, and having learned it to practice it in the interests of suffering and dying humanity."

"Mental healing" in this case, according to their theory, would consist in getting rid of the idea of sin, sickness and death. But as a matter of fact, the idea is not identical with sin, sickness and death; and, therefore, even if you succeed in ignoring sin, the sin remains, unless it is repented for and forgiven. Mrs. Eddy tried hard to ignore death, but in spite of this she died Dec. 4, 1910. The fallacy of their reasoning is apparent. They advise people to fight a phantom, to destroy something unreal, and to look upon actual things and occurrences as mere delusions of mortal mind.

Under the guise of mind, they idolize the body. I have perused their literature: "Science and Health with Key to the Scriptures;" "Christian Science Sentinel," a weekly magazine; "The Christian Science Monitor," a daily paper; and the tracts "True Orthodoxy;" "Brotherhood of Man;" "How Should the Sick Be Healed;" "Christian Science Business Life;" "The True Law;" "Lessons from a Workshop;" "Healing the Sick;" "There Is Rest and Peace on Earth;" and "The Real and the Unreal;" but I fail to find any passage treating of virtue, on how to serve God, on self-denial, or penance, or on anything whatsoever which brings the soul nearer to God. The whole lesson taught by them is: idolize your body; take care of the body, but avoid the physician and refuse medicine; be your own doctor by concentrating your thoughts upon the idea that sin, death and matter is all a delusion; or as the foundress of "Christian Science" puts it: "When the Science of

Church of Christ, Scientist

Being is understood, every man will be his own physician, and Truth will be the universal panacea." Science and Health with Key to the Scriptures, P. 38.

Their tenets are anti-christian and absolutely materialistic. All they retain of Christianity is the name, the misnomer: Christian Science. Sacraments and other means of grace are unknown in their teachings.

But one thing can be said to their credit: their literature is pure. They are supporting a clean daily, their own Christian Science Monitor. They are making great propaganda for their cult and distribute their literature most liberally among the people. This means liberal contributions on the part of their members, who are eager to disseminate "Christian Science" tenets. That many of them are sincere cannot be questioned.

Questions on the Text

1. What are some of the unchristian teachings of the Adventists?
2. What date did they set for the end of the world?
3. How do they err on Hell?
4. What does Jesus teach concerning the reprobates?
5. How many centuries after Christ did this visionary folly of Adventists spring into existence?
6. Who was John Alexander Dowie?
7. In what century did the Dowieites make their appearance?
8. They spurn the physician; what does God tell us about the physician?
9. Who is the founder of the Salvation Army?
10. How many years after Christ did the Salvation Army appear?

Christian Denominations

11. When and where did the Mormons originate?
12. When was the Book of Mormons published?
13. What is the main fallacy of the Universalists?
14. Can they have any shadow of a claim to have Jesus for their founder?
15. Who started Unitarianism?
16. How did Jesus prove His divinity?
17. Can a Christian be a Unitarian?
18. Who is the founder of the Church of the New Jerusalem?
19. When did this heretical novelty get a footing?
20. What specifically Christian doctrine did Swedenborg deny?
21. In what branches of learning does he betray his lamentable ignorance?
22. Who is the foundress of Christian Science?
23. When did it come into the world?
24. What is their vaunted Mental Healing?

Concluding Remarks

THERE is only one Church which dates back to the time of Jesus Christ, the Redeemer of the World. It is the Catholic Church, of which St. Peter was the first Head as visible representative of Christ. When Jesus, the Good Shepherd, was about to withdraw His visible presence from this earth, He gave His entire flock over to Simon Peter, and instructed St. Peter to feed His lambs and His sheep. Simon Peter was the first Pope of the Church, the Father of Christianity. An unbroken line of successors of St. Peter in the office as Head of the Church extends through all the centuries of the Christian era. As we have seen in the forepart of this book, under the heading "The Catholic Church" the teachings of Jesus Christ and the means of grace instituted by Him have been handed down through the ages even unto our time.

This Church is the one that Jesus established. It is holy in its Founder, for the Son of God established it. It is holy in its mission, for the Son of God endowed it with supernatural means of grace. It is holy in its members, for it has produced millions of saints, whose sanctity God attested by unquestionable miracles. It is holy in its purpose, for it aims at the sanctification of mankind. God is serving mankind and He asks mankind to serve Him. He promised us a Heaven, an eternal reward, for our fidelity and His service.

As our Savior was persecuted, so is the Church He founded. This Jesus predicted: "Remember my word that I said to you: The servant is not greater than his master. If they have persecuted me, they will also persecute you: if they have kept my word, they will keep yours also." St. John 15:20.

Enemies from within the Church and from without have turned their efforts against the Church through the various centuries. Their aim was to destroy it. But the Church which Jesus founded, the Catholic Church, has withstood all these attacks. Jesus had predicted this on the day when Simon Peter publicly professed his belief in the divinity of Christ. Jesus said: "I say to thee: That thou art Peter; and upon this rock I will build my church, and *the gates of hell shall not* prevail against it." Matt. 16:18.

If you are a member of this Church, thank God for this grace and privilege. If you are not as yet a member, pray to the Holy Ghost for the light of faith, that it may lead you on unto the membership of this Church. Remember this is the only Church that Jesus Christ founded, the only Church that comes from God and that can lead you to God.

Index

Index

A

Advent Christians	194
Adventists	193
African M. E. Church	187
African M. E. Zion Church	187
African Union M. P. Church	187
Age-to-come Adventist	195
Ambrose, St.	77
Anabaptists	154
Anglican Church	136
Anglican Orders	141
Anti-Mission Baptists	172
Antiquity Argument	58
Apologetic Writer	38
Apostles, the Names	26
Apostolic Constitution	84
Apostolicity Argument	66
Associated Presbyterians	147
Athanasius, St.	48
Augustine, St.	54

B

Baptism, Sacrament	68
Baptist Church	162
Basil, St.	51
Bible Christians	187
Bible Translations	119
Biddle, John	219
Blessed Virgin Mary	95
Bohemian Brethren	176
Booth, William	206

	PAGE
Brief Synopsis of Catholic Doctrine	103
Brigham Young	211
Broad Church	140
Brown, Robert	149

C

Caerularius	112
Caesarius, St.	82
Calvin, John	142
Calvin's Assertions	144
Campbellites	173
Catholic Church	25
Catholic Church the True Church	107
Christ Jesus, Founder of the Catholic Church	25
Christ Jesus, the Son of God	25
Christian Catholic Church of Zion	196
Christian Science	228
Christians	173
Chronological List of Popes	63
Chrysologus, St. Peter	81
Chrysostom, St.	77
Church of Christ, Scientists	228
Church of England	136
Church of God, Adventist	194
Church of God, Baptist	173
Church of New Jerusalem	222
Clement, St.	34
Colored M. E. Church	187
Concluding Remarks	233
Confirmation, Sacrament	72
Congregational Church	149
Congregational Methodists	186
Consent, Argument	58
Cyprian, St.	44

Index

	PAGE
Cyril of Alexandria, St.	99
Cyril of Jerusalem, St.	71

D

Didache	69
Disciples	173
Dowie, John Alexander	196
Dowieites	196
Dunkards	171

E

Eddy, Mrs. Mary Baker	228
Eddyism	228
Ephraem, St.	52
Epiphanius, St.	86
Episcopal Church	136
Eucharist, Sacrament	73
Eusebius	47
Evangelical Adventists	193
Extreme Unction, Sacrament	82

F

Fox, George	179
Free Baptists	171
Free Methodists	186
Friends	179

G

General Baptists	170
German Baptists	171
Greek Orthodox Church	112
Gregory of Nazianzus, St.	98

H

| Hard Shell Baptists | 172 |

	PAGE
Henry VIII Against Luther	120
Hicksite Quaker	181
High Church	139
Hilary, St.	50
Holy Orders, Sacrament	83

I

Ignatius, St.	35
Independent Methodists	187
Innocent Pope, St.	73
Introduction	v
Irenaeus, St.	39

J

Jerome, St.	53
Jesus, the Son of God	17
Jesus Christ, Founder of Catholic Church	25
Justin, St.	38

K

Kingdom Movement of Zion	199
Knox, John	142

L

Lactantius	46
Latter Day Saints	209
Life of Advent Union	195
Linsley, Theophilus	219
Low Church	139
Luther and Bible Translation	119
Luther, Martin	115
Lutheran Church	115

M

Mary, the Mother of God	95
Mass, Sacrifice	88
Matrimony, Sacrament	85
Maximus, St.	87
Menno Simonis	159
Mennonite Church	159
Methodist Church	182
Methodist Episcopal	185
Methodist Protestant	186
Miller, William	193
Moravians	176
Mormons	209
Murray, John	216

N

New Congregational Methodists	187
New School Presbyterians	147
Nilus, St.	78
Northern Presbyterians	147

O

Old School Baptists	172
Old School Presbyterians	147
Old Two-Seed, etc., Baptists	173
Orders Holy, Sacrament	83
Origen	41
Orthodox Greek Church	112
Orthodox Quakers	181

P

Pacian, St.	71
Particular Baptist	171
Penance, Sacrament	79

Peter Chrysologus, St.	81
Photius	112
Physician and Bible	204
Pilgrim Fathers	150
Polycarp, St.	37
Popes, List of	63
Presbyterian Church	142
Primitive Baptists	172
Primitive Methodists	187
Primitive Quakers	181
Puritans	149

Q

Quakers	179

R

Reasoning Leads to God, Sound	4
Reformed Presbyterians	147
Regular Presbyterians	147
Relly, James	216
Ritualists	139

S

Sacrifice of the Mass	88
Salvation Army	206
Scientists, Eddyists	228
Separate Baptists	172
Seven Sacraments	68
Seventh Day Adventists	194
Seventh Day Baptists	171
Six-Principle Baptists	171
Smith, Joseph	209
Smyth, John	163
Sound Reasoning Leads to God	4
Statistics on Religions in the World Today	1
Storch, Nicholas	154
Swedenborg, Emanuel	222

T

Tertullian	42
Theodoret	79
Theodotus	100
Testimony of Early Father	33
Tractarian Movement	139
Translations of the Bible	119

U

Union American M. E. Church	187
Unitarians	219
United Baptists	173
United Brethren	188
United Methodist Free Church	187
Universalists	216
Universality, Argument	58

V

Vincent of Lerin, St.	56
Virgin Mary	95

W

Welsh Calvinistic Methodists	187
Wesley, Charles	182
Wesley, John	182
Wesleyan Methodist	182
Wesleyan Methodist Connection	186
White, Mrs.	194
Whitefield, George	182
Wilburites	181
Williams, Roger	170
Winebrennerians	173

Z

Zinzendorf, Count Louis	176
Zion Union Apostolic Church	187